A Trilogy of
CHRISTMAS PLAYS
for Children

A Trilogy of Christmas Plays for Children

Carol Preston

Music selected by John Langstaff

Illustrated with music, photographs, and diagrams

Harcourt, Brace & World, Inc., New York

38941

PN
6120
A5
P785

B. 6.69

Library of Congress Catalog Card Number: 67-17157

Printed in the United States of America

The author and the publisher wish to thank the following for permission to reprint the selections listed below:

BOOSEY AND HAWKES, INC., *for an excerpt from the first verse and melody line of "The Christ Child's Lullaby" from SONGS OF THE HEBRIDES, Vol. I, Copyright 1909 by Boosey & Co., Renewed 1936, noted in Eriskay from the singing of Mrs. John Macinnes, words from Father Allan MacDonald, and arranged with pianoforte accompaniment by Marjory Kennedy-Fraser; and for an excerpt from the first verse and melody line of the "Sussex Mummers' Carol" reprinted in the OXFORD BOOK OF CAROLS (No. 45), Oxford University Press, London, from Lucy E. Broadwood's ENGLISH TRADITIONAL SONGS AND CAROLS, Copyright 1908 by Boosey & Co., Renewed 1936.*

EDITIONS COSTALLAT, *60, Chaussée d'Antin, Paris 9 ème, for "Hosanna" from L'ENFANCE DU CHRIST by Berlioz.*

J. FISCHER & BRO. *for the last verse and melody line of "The Cherry Tree Carol" arranged by Hilton Rufty; for an excerpt from the first verse and melody line of "Wondrous Love," arranged by Annabel Buchanan, and for an excerpt from the first verse and melody line of "The Babe of Bethlehem," arranged by John Powell — both from TWELVE FOLK HYMNS edited by John Powell.*

GALAXY MUSIC CORPORATION *for an excerpt from the first verse and melody line of "Nova, Nova" from MUSICA BRITANNICA, Vol. IV, Stainer & Bell Ltd., London, (Galaxy Music Corporation, U. S. agent); for an excerpt from the melody line and words of "Go Tell It on the Mountain," arranged by John W. Work; and for an excerpt from the melody line and words of the "Ancient Moravian Christmas Carol," arranged by Harvey Gaul.*

THE H. W. GRAY COMPANY, INC., *for an excerpt from the melody line and words of "My Shepherd Will Supply My Need," arranged by Virgil Thompson.*

DR. MAUD KARPELES, O.B.E., *literary executor and agent for the Cecil Sharp Estate, for the "Apple Tree Wassail" collected by Cecil J. Sharp.*

PHILIP MERRILL, *Music Director of the Country Dance Society, Inc., for his variants of the Appalachian folk tunes, "Soldier Boy" and "Charlie's Sweet," used as accompaniments to the dances.*

NOVELLO & COMPANY LTD. *for an excerpt from the melody line and words of "The Moon Shines Bright" and for an excerpt from the melody line and words of "The Virgin Unspotted"—both from FOLK-SONG CAROLS, collected and arranged by Cecil J. Sharp.*

OXFORD UNIVERSITY PRESS, London, *for verse four and the melody line of the "Sussex Carol" (No. 24); for an excerpt from the melody line and words of the "Coventry Carol" (No. 22); for an excerpt from the first verse and melody line of the "Gloucestershire Wassail" (No. 31); for verse eight of "Song of the Crib" (No. 77), which appears as dialogue on page 90, lines 9–12; for two verses of "Rocking" (No. 87), which appear as dialogue on page 89, lines 18–21 and lines 23–27; and for verse five of "Waking-Time" (No. 88), which appears as dialogue on page 90, lines 15–21 — all reprinted from THE OXFORD BOOK OF CAROLS.*

E. C. SCHIRMER MUSIC COMPANY *for an excerpt from the melody line and words of "Lo, How a Rose," a sixteenth century melody harmonized by Praetorius; for an excerpt from the melody line and words of "Upon My Lap My Sov'reign Sits" by Martin Peerson; for an excerpt from the melody line and words of "Ding-Dong! Merrily on High," melody Branle de L'Official (from Thoinot Arbeau's Orchesographie, 1588); and for an excerpt from the melody line and words of "Star in the East" (Hail the blest morn), based on a Kentucky version of the folk-hymn, as sung by Mrs. Rachel Ritchie — all four selections used with permission of the copyright owners, E. C. Schirmer Music Company, Boston.*

G. SCHIRMER, INC., *for an excerpt from the melody line and words of "Masters in This Hall," Copyright by J. Curwen & Sons, London.*

STAINER & BELL LTD., *Lesbourne Road, Reigate, Surrey, England, for the melody line and verse one of "This Is the Truth" arranged by R. Vaughan Williams.*

TO
THE CHILDREN OF THE POTOMAC SCHOOL
and
THEIR TEACHERS
who together made these plays
a beloved part of the school tradition
and to
Helen M. Seth-Smith
without whom they could never have been given

Contents

INTRODUCTION

"This is the truth sent from above"—in the darkened room the words of the old carol float out in the clear tones of the angel chorus. On the stage the shepherds, complaining of the cold and wet, are huddled around a fire when suddenly they see an unknown star shining in the sky and hear angels sing of the birth of the long-promised Christ Child. In a stable lit only by the light of the wondrous Babe and the star, they find Him lying in the arms of His mother singing to Him, "Lully, lulla, thou little tiny child." Joseph, leaning on his staff, stands guard, while the ox and the ass kneel close to keep the little Virgin and the Baby "warm with their sweet breath." The shepherds offer their gifts—a bird, a crook, a sprig of holly. The audience is very quiet as the old miracle lives again in the intensity of this innocent beauty. So the Christmas play at The Potomac School was for many years.

When I first went there as head, I cast about for a play that would be the simple enactment of the Christmas story with the directness, vigor, and imagination appropriate to children. Mary Berkeley, a fifth-grade teacher, knew an old folk tale about animals on Christmas Eve that offered a suitable framework. Anne Malcolmson, an English teacher with a knowledge of Middle English, put it into script form and incorporated lines and phrases from several medieval miracle or mystery plays, primarily from *The Second Shepherds Play of the Townley Cycle*. This joint effort, together with some of the loveliest carols, gave us exactly what we had hoped for. As the school—and the potential cast—grew in size, a Prologue was added to the original text based on the King James Version of the Bible.

As time went on, we developed two more plays. Sparked by Lauren Ford's lovely book, *The Ageless Story*, I gave one an American setting through scenery, costumes, and American carols. Selections from the King James Version of the Bible gave us the text.

For the third play, I again turned to the English miracle plays. Although *The Nativity Play of the York Cycle* performed by the Thatchers Guild gave the principal theme (Lucy Tomlin Smith, main source), I used excerpts from other cycles, feeling it permissible to do so since originally the towns borrowed freely from one another. Herman Daimling was my chief source for the Chester plays, as was G. England for the Townley Cycle. I used nothing from Coventry except the famous carol. The authorities agree that while these miracle or mystery plays parallel those of France and other countries of Europe, the likeness is due to the fact that they used the same source for their stories—the Bible. The character and interpretation came from contemporary life, in the case of these plays, that of England.

Emerging from the restrictions of the Middle Ages, these old plays came "into full flower" in the mid-fourteenth and fifteenth centuries when humanism was astir in England. Physically, the plays moved from the church to the street, where they came under the strong secular influence of the guilds, each of which was responsible for the preservation and acting of a particular play. Still regarded as a cycle depicting man's life in the great scheme from creation to the last trump, they gained in vigor as the characters escaped from stylized rigidity to become three-dimensional human individuals. Full of faults (Mack was a famous sheep-stealer and Herod a terror), they also showed people of nobility; robust humor was mixed with reverence. The shepherds often seem near to the mechanics in *A Midsummer Night's Dream*. The audience was revealed to itself in these little "mirrors held up to nature," and so the plays developed into folk art, although some of the finest poetry was composed by individuals.

The humanistic wave that gathered force five hundred years ago was of such strength that we are still carried along by it. In spite of technology, we look to man as ultimately responsible for himself. In this sense the mystery plays are contemporary and expressive of us. We still groan over "heavy taxings," grumble about the weather, and sing of love and death. Perhaps most adults have lost the sense of wonder that envisions miracles as a necessary part of life, although many children accept them naturally.

At the same time that the mystery plays were reaching their peak, carols—"those masterpieces of tantalizing symplicity"—began to pour forth in song and dance. Their poetry matched or surpassed that of the plays. The music was buoyant, to be danced to. The human conception of Christ as playing ball or being punished by His mother for disobedience was in contrast to the medieval character and mood of the liturgical plain song. The carols reflected every phase of life, truthfully, without sentimentality.

In adapting these plays, we so intermingled the carols with the spoken word that together they form the whole. Although "The Coventry Carol" is the only one that we know surely was used in these plays, there must have been others. They fit so happily that we feel it a restoration rather than a departure to bring play and carol together again. Going back to the original meaning of the word carol, we used some of them as accompaniments to dances, which are also based on appropriate folk material.

We have been fortunate in having John Langstaff, the head of the music department at The Potomac School, to select and direct the music, for he is not only a fine musician, but also a person with unusual knowledge of traditional material coupled with discriminating taste. He so taught the carols that for those who have sung them and for us who have heard them, they have become forever part of our heritage of the beauty of Christmas.

Old Christmas, In a Manger Laid, and *Born in a Stable* became our trilogy of plays, one given in each successive year. They are variations on the theme, distinct yet in a sense the same, a kind of Christmas fugue.

Simplicity is the keynote to the plays and their production, but simplicity requires care in detail that the grace of the children and the directness of the poetry may not be marred. At The Potomac School, ten-year-olds were chosen to give the plays, although they are suitable for any age that can play the parts with unself-consciousness, natural dignity, and humor. The older children there composed the "angel chorus" to sing the carols.

The plays are so presented here that they may be used with flexibility and adapted to the needs of a particular group, churches, clubs, or other schools. Suggestions are made with great care so that the quality remains the same should expansion or contraction be necessary to suit the numbers available, but it will be understood that flexibility is not distortion.

From the beginning, we decided at The Potomac School not to turn the plays over to a drama department but to consider them the common responsibility of many teachers and all of the children. So, running through the minds, imagination, and work of the hands of many of us, the Christmas plays over the years have become a beloved part of the school tradition. In a true sense, they were not so much plays as celebrations in which all participated, each doing his best to make as lovely a Christmas gift as possible to one another and to those who had gone before, for former students and parents made a point of coming back to the Christmas plays that linked the past and present. We found it true that "in our traditions we are all one."

For the benefit of those in schools where finding time for anything "extra" like a play is always difficult, we would say that the school life was enriched and through intelligent administration there was a minimum of dislocation. Three weeks was the time allowed in the school calendar for rehearsals and production, although learning the carols began earlier, in the regular music periods. Free times, assembly periods, and art classes for work on scenery were carefully scheduled so that there was little use of academic periods and confusion was avoided. For the fifth grade, the play was an important part of their English curriculum.

The plays served as a stimulus to many activities. During several years, children carved figures for a crèche that looked like a "primitive." Now set up each season, it has become a Christmas treasure. Three successive sixth-grade classes studying the Middle Ages depicted one of the plays in a needlepoint "tapestry," worthy of the thirteenth century. That, too, is now eagerly looked for each Christmastime. In the art room, nativity pictures were painted and decorated the walls of the school. In English classes, poems were written, the words of the old carols learned, and indeed there was no end to what the imagination and ingenuity of teachers and children devised in response to this moment of heightened feeling when Christmas was in our bones. Teaching and learning were strengthened when teachers and children throughout the school were brought together in creative activity.

For the benefit of others perhaps not experienced in giving such plays with children, practical and technical information is given by those members of the teaching staff at The Potomac School who were directly connected with the production over a period of time. There are sections on directing, music, construction of a stage, costumes, lighting, etc. Throughout the text, the numbers following the name of each carol refer to the Suggested List of Appropriate Music and Its Use for Each Play. These will be found in the Appendix.

To name all of the teachers and children who have worked on the plays with skill and enjoyment would be a roll call of the school during the past twenty-five years. To certain individuals who have contributed their gifts in special areas with sustained effort comes acknowledgment and appreciation, not only for *what* they have given, but also for their imagination and generosity in giving.

Assisting Mr. Langstaff with the music have been his wife, Nancy, and Mrs. Leonide Ourusoff, who, as well as teaching and accompanying the singing, has worked endlessly in sorting and writing out carols for this book. A delightful addition to the music has been the school orchestra and bell ringing under the skilled direction of Robert Henderson. William H. Old, Jr., has taken the fine photographs that enliven the book. Peppino Mangravite, distinguished artist and teacher, who has for years directed the art at The Potomac School, worked with unfailing perception and sensitivity in helping teachers and children to understand the whole. John Hebeler, head of the art department, worked with the ninth grade year after year to design and paint original scenery to suit each play as it was given. May Gadd, Director of the Country Dance Society of America, composed out of her long experience dances based on traditional material and, like the music, appropriate in its grace, vigor, and origin. Helen Fox, with the help of Faith Marr, evolved costumes unbelievably lovely in line and color; Irving Seeley possessed extraordinary ingenuity in making properties; Diana King developed beautiful lighting that held the whole play in luminuous simplicity; Newell Price, now assistant head of the school, and Elsie Archer, without whose help anything in the Upper School would have been impossible, had charge of the angel chorus; Caroline Seamans, head of the Middle School, which included the fifth grade, with her enthusiasm, understanding, and capacity for making "the crooked places straight," made the rehearsals and all they entailed run smoothly. Helping her and me have been the fifth-grade teachers with their intimate knowledge of the children. Eleanor Barlow not only helped with the production but also with her gift for exquisite calligraphy autographed the three carols prefacing each of the plays. Without Miss Seth-Smith, assistant head of the school when I was head, there could have been no plays. From first to last, she was there at every turn, helping, advising, consulting. She took care of plans for the erection of scenery and worked out the multiplicity of details as they affected the school as a whole. The success of the plays depended in no small degree on the happiness and good humor she always engendered in those around her, something so necessary to the efficiency that always marked her work. Beside her stood Wilton Boyle, Superintendent of Buildings and Grounds. Nor could what we have done ever have been put together had it not been for the patient typing and re-typing by Louise Nuttycombe, to whom I am most grateful. To my happy lot fell the "construction" of two of the plays and the direction of all of them for over twenty-five years.

This may sound like a great many people, and the plays could have been produced by a far smaller number, but we dovetailed jobs, and things fell so naturally into place that it became a time, as I said, of happy involvement for us all.

Along with appreciation to those who have helped in the past, best wishes go to those who may give these plays in the future. We hope that in working intimately with chil-dren, in learning this poetry, singing these carols, you, too, may feel Christmas very near—and our comradeship who have loved these plays before you.

Carol Preston
Windwhistle Hill
Great Falls, Virginia

GENERAL NOTES

1. As many people (children) as are available, preferably older than those in the cast, compose the chorus.

2. Carols are sung by the chorus unless otherwise noted.

3. Carols used in these plays are numbered for reference in the text and are keyed to the Suggested List of Appropriate Music and Its Use for Each Play in the Appendix. They can, if necessary, be cut in number.

4. If a chorus is not available, the carols can be played on the piano, or parents and audience may sing a few carols before and after the play and perhaps a Gloria when the shepherds see the angels.

5. The Virgin sings her own lullaby unaccompanied.

6. Just before each play begins, the audience sings "The First Noël,"[1] during which the chorus enters quickly in the dark and, as the members take their places, joins in the singing. If possible, the chorus carries a descant during the last verse.

7. Where a chorus or instruments are not available, there are listed in the Appendix some records that can be cut by the use of a tape recorder and the music inserted at appropriate places.

Old Christmas

On Christmas Night

Traditional Carol from England

All out of dark-ness we have light,

Which made the An-gels sing this night:

All out of dark-ness we have light,

Which made the An-gels sing this night:

"Glo-ry to God and Peace to Men,

Now and for-ev-er more. A-men."

Old Christmas

CAST OF CHARACTERS

The Prophecy

    MOURNFUL PEOPLE (*six*)

    ANGELS (*two—may be from the* CRÈCHE ANGELS)

    PROPHETS (*six*)

    MARY

    GABRIEL

The Fulfillment

    ANGELS OF THE CRÈCHE (*six*)

    SHEPHERDS (*six*)

    COCK

    RAVEN

    ASS

    OX

    LAMB

    MELCHIOR, BALTHASAR, *and* CASPAR, *the Three Kings*

    ATTENDANTS (*three*)

    ARCHANGELS (*two*)

    MARY

JOSEPH

GREEN MEN OF THE WINTER SOLSTICE (*six*)

CHORUS

ORCHESTRA

NOTE: More shepherds may be added by dividing some speeches or by allowing those with non-speaking parts to make gifts.

MELCHIOR, BALTHASAR, CASPAR, the three ATTENDANTS, and the six GREEN MEN OF THE WINTER SOLSTICE may be omitted if a smaller cast is necessary.

THE PROPHECY

SCENE: *During the singing of the carol, "Veni Emmanuel" (first verse)*[2], *enter six* MOURNFUL PEOPLE *who so group themselves in the center before the curtains as to indicate great sorrow. They are followed by two* ANGELS *who stand "unseen" behind them, hands folded. Enter three* PROPHETS *from each side, who stand on raised levels. Variety in voices is effective in what is almost an antiphonal lamentation before the* PROPHETS *speak.*

FIRST PERSON: Upon the summer fruits and upon the harvest the battle shout is fallen.

SECOND PERSON: And gladness is taken away, and joy out of the fields. And in the country there shall be no singing, neither joyful noise.

THIRD PERSON: The very hills do tremble; the land is burnt up; the people also are as fuel or fire; no man spareth his brother.

FIRST PERSON: Behold, the Lord maketh the earth empty. All joy is darkened—the mirth of the land is gone.

FOURTH PERSON: Jehovah hath forsaken me, the Lord hath forsaken me.

FIFTH PERSON: How shall I comfort thee? It is a day of perplexity, a breaking down of walls, and a crying to the mountains.

FOURTH PERSON: We grope for the wall like the blind; we look for light, but we behold darkness.

FIRST PERSON: The grass withereth, the flower fadeth, because the breath of the Lord bloweth upon it. Surely the people is grass!

FIRST ANGEL: The grass withereth, the flower fadeth, but the word of our God shall stand forever.

FOURTH PERSON: The anger of the Lord is kindled against His people, and He hath stretched forth His hand against them and smitten them.

SECOND ANGEL: Lord, Thy hand is lifted up, yet they see not.

(CHORUS *sings second verse of "Veni Emmanuel."* [2])

FIRST PROPHET: Comfort ye, comfort ye, my people. Holy, holy, holy is the Lord of Hosts; the whole earth is full of His Glory.

SECOND PROPHET: There shall come forth a rod out of the stem of Jesse, and a branch shall grow out of his roots. And the spirit of the Lord shall rest upon Him, and the spirit of wisdom and understanding. And with righteousness shall He judge the people. And the root of Jesse will stand as an ensign to the people.

THIRD PROPHET: The Lord Himself shall give you a sign. Behold, a virgin shall bear a son and shall call his name Emmanuel.

(*Sing four verses of the Annunciation carol, "Nova, Nova."* [3])

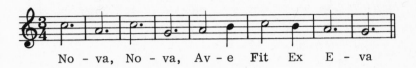

No - va, No - va, Av - e Fit Ex E - va

As the carol of the Annunciation begins, the two ANGELS *hold open the curtains in the center sufficiently to reveal* MARY *sitting against a panel painted to represent a picture frame of flowers. At the same moment, the people fall back kneeling at the feet of the* PROPHETS *at the two sides. If no curtains are used,* MARY *walks quietly to the center reading.* GABRIEL *enters from the other side with a swift, rhythmic movement. All look at pantomime of carol by* MARY *and* GABRIEL. *It is as though they see a vision. What follows flows from it.* ANGELS *close curtains. See the section on the Dances.)*

FOURTH PROPHET: The people that walked in darkness have seen a great light.

FIFTH PROPHET: The wolf also shall dwell with the lamb; and the leopard shall lie down with the kid; and the calf and the young lion and the fatling together. And the cow and the bear shall feed; their young ones shall lie down together; and the lion shall eat straw like the ox; and a little *child* shall lead them.

SIXTH PROPHET: He shall feed His flock like a shepherd; And He shall gather the lambs in His arm.
And carry them in His bosom,
And shall gently lead those that are with young.

SIXTH PERSON (*with joy and awe steps to center of stage looking up with arms raised*):
For unto us a Child is born;
Unto us a son is given
And the government shall be upon His shoulder
And His name shall be called Wonderful, Counsellor,
Mighty God, Everlasting Father, Prince of Peace.

(ANGELS *again hold back the curtains, and* PEOPLE *exit through the center, followed by the* PROPHETS *and then the* ANGELS—*all with a look of hope and faith.* CHORUS *sings first verse of "Puer Nobis."* [4])

THE FULFILLMENT

TIME: *The First Christmas Eve foretold by the prophets*
SCENE: *As the curtains open,* CHORUS *sings the first and fourth verses of the "Sussex Carol,"* [5] *frequently known as "On Christmas Night."*

A frosty field surrounds a barn at the center back, two steps up with closed doors. Three ANGELS *(invisible to* SHEPHERDS*) are on either side of the stable—as though hanging in the sky—playing instruments. There should be a soft spotlight on the* ANGELS*—a soft light but enough for good visibility on the stage. A group of six* SHEPHERDS *stands in the center, huddled with cold.* OX, LAMB, ASS, RAVEN, *and* COCK *are also huddled at the right back.*

FIRST SHEPHERD: Ah, but the cold wind whistles through my tatters!

SECOND SHEPHERD: Yea, 'tis no new thing, I trow. My fingers are chapped from holding the crook these many winters!

FIRST SHEPHERD: Lord, but this frost is sharp. It makes my eyes to water and my shoes freeze to my feet.

THIRD SHEPHERD: Come, lads, settle yourselves and sleep. Your grumbling brings but poor cheer to our hearts.

SECOND SHEPHERD: There was never since Noah's Flood such floods seen or winds and rains so rude and storms so keen.

FOURTH SHEPHERD: See how our beasts huddle together

29

for warmth. 'Tis a bitter night. Since morn I have run in the mire. I'm cold and will build a fire.

(*Two go off to get a little wood to build a fire around which they gather.*)

FIFTH SHEPHERD: Cease thy chattering. 'Twill be morn soon enough. Then will the cock crow and our dreams be shattered. Peace now, sleep!

(*They settle themselves. The* ox *lows, the* LAMB *bleats, the* ASS *brays.*)

FIRST SHEPHERD: Lord, what a clatter do those beasts make!

THIRD SHEPHERD: And thou, too, silly one. Go to sleep.

(*The* RAVEN *caws; the* COCK *crows.*)

SECOND SHEPHERD: See, thy grumbling hath aroused the cock.

(*Goes over to see that beasts are all right—quiets them.*)

SIXTH SHEPHERD: The beasts would urge us all to sleep. Hush, lads. Let them speak to us in our dreams.

FOURTH SHEPHERD: My grandam saith that one day the beasts shall speak in our tongue.

FIFTH SHEPHERD: When, pray, is this to be?

FOURTH SHEPHERD: 'Tis but a tale of my grandam.

SECOND SHEPHERD: Tell it! By my faith I cannot sleep on this hard, cold ground.

THIRD SHEPHERD: Yea, the night will be long. Tell thy tale, lad.

FOURTH SHEPHERD: My grandam saith that the Messias shall be born to save men from their sins.

FIFTH SHEPHERD: 'Twas not thy grandam, boy! Isaiah 'twas foretold it.

(CHORUS *sings a cappella two lines of "Lo, How a Rose."* [6]

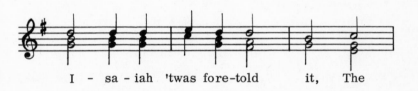

I - sa - iah 'twas fore-told it, The

rose I have in mind,

CHORUS *continues to hum the next two lines as* FOURTH SHEPHERD *interrupts.*)

FOURTH SHEPHERD: Yea, but my grandam saith further that on the night of His coming the beasts themselves, even the ox and the ass, shall speak with the tongues of men.

(*The* LAMB *bleats and the* OX *lows.*)

SIXTH SHEPHERD: Thy grandam is a foolish woman. The lamb and the ox bid thee cease thy chatter.

FOURTH SHEPHERD: 'Twas a wise woman told her that

one day the beasts shall speak. (*Pause*)

SECOND SHEPHERD (*wonderingly*): When think you the Messias will be born?

THIRD SHEPHERD: On such a night as this mayhap.

SECOND SHEPHERD: Not in our time, I trow. Shall not hap in our time aught but the rain and the woe and these heavy taxings.

SIXTH SHEPHERD: We that walk of nights our cattle to keep, we see startling sights when other men sleep.

FIFTH SHEPHERD: Cease thy silly chatterings. Come, lads, sleep.

(FIRST SHEPHERD *plays pipe while slowly the other* SHEPHERDS *settle themselves and sleep.*

CHORUS *sings softly first verse of "The Moon Shines Bright,"* [7] *collected and arranged by Cecil J. Sharp.*

The   moon   shines bright   and   the

stars give a light, a   lit - tle be-fore it is day

CHORUS *sings triumphantly the fourth verse of the "Sussex Carol" or "Alleluia Round."* [5] *The light in the star comes on.* COCK, RAVEN, ASS, OX, *and* LAMB *stir themselves then with great excitement.*)

COCK (*stretches and gives clarion call immediately*):
Cock-a-doodle-do! Christ the Lord is born! Christ the Lord is born!

(*Each of the following animals makes his characteristic noise melt into the sound of the words.*)

RAVEN: Caw! Caw! When? When?

ASS: Eyah! Eyah! This night! This night!

OX (*lows*): M-Where? M-Where?

LAMB: Baa! Baa! Bethlehem! Bethlehem!

(SHEPHERDS *wake, sit up, startled, and face downstage.*)

SIXTH SHEPHERD (*in awe*): Hark, didst hear the beasts?

FIFTH SHEPHERD: Ay, but these be learnèd fowl.

THIRD SHEPHERD: Didst hear the ass say that the Messias is born this night?

FOURTH SHEPHERD: 'Tis as my grandam saith. (*Jumps up.*)

SECOND SHEPHERD: Sh-h! They speak again.

COCK: Cock-a-doodle-do! Christ the Lord is born! Christ the Lord is born!

RAVEN: Caw! Caw! When? When?

ASS: Eyah! Eyah! This night! This night!

OX: M-Where? M-Where?

LAMB: Bethlehem! Bethlehem!

(CHORUS OF ANGELS *sings first verse of "While By My Sheep."* [8] SHEPHERDS *look in awe and amazement.*)

ANGEL OF THE CRÈCHE: Fear not! For behold, I bring you good tidings of great joy, which shall be to all people. For unto you is born this day in the city of David, a Saviour, which is Christ the Lord. And this shall be a sign unto you; ye shall find the Babe wrapped in swaddling clothes and lying in a manger.

(CHORUS *sings second verse of "While By My Sheep."* [8])

FIRST SHEPHERD: 'Twas as fine a song as ever I heard.

SECOND SHEPHERD: What were these tidings which the angels have brought?

FIFTH SHEPHERD: My eyes smart from the vision.

SIXTH SHEPHERD: 'Tis as thy grandam hath said. The Messias is born.

FOURTH SHEPHERD: The beasts themselves have told us this miracle.

THIRD SHEPHERD: Where shall we seek this Babe?

LAMB: Bethlehem, Bethlehem.

FIRST SHEPHERD: Let us go to Him!

(SHEPHERDS *see star.*)

ASS: Tonight! Tonight!

SIXTH SHEPHERD: Hie we thither then speedily, though we be wet and weary, to that Child and that Lady. We must not lose those joys.

FOURTH SHEPHERD: Let us bear gifts, even such poor things as we can share.

(*Exit* SHEPHERDS. CHORUS *sings first two verses of "Sing Aloud on This Day!"*[9] *and during the second verse enter* CASPAR, BALTHASAR, MELCHIOR, *and* ATTENDANTS *from audience.*)

COCK: Christ the Lord is born! Christ the Lord is born!

(CASPAR, BALTHASAR, *and* MELCHIOR *astonished by beasts.*)

MELCHIOR: 'Tis at last the birth of the King of Kings! Dost hear the cock?

BALTHASAR: When is this wondrous thing come to pass?

RAVEN: When? When?

ASS: Tonight! Tonight!

CASPAR: Where is He that is born King of the Jews? For we have seen His star in the East and are come to worship Him.

OX: Where? Where?

LAMB: Bethlehem! Bethlehem!

FIRST ATTENDANT: The place is near at hand.

SECOND ATTENDANT: When I see Him and feel, I shall know full well it is true as steel what the prophets have spoken.

THIRD ATTENDANT: It is a marvel thus to be stirred with dread.

MELCHIOR: To Bethlehem they bade that we should go. I am sore afraid we tarry too slow.

(As CASPAR, BALTHASAR, *and* MELCHIOR *exit on the opposite side of the stage from the* SHEPHERDS, CHORUS *sings as a round or in unison:*

Anonymous Round

For us a Child is born this day, Al -

le - - lu - ya, Al - le -lu - ya.

CHORUS *sings the third verse of "Sing Aloud on This Day!"* [9] *Lights go down, leaving only a glimmer on the* CRÈCHE ANGELS. CHORUS *sings two verses of "Upon My Lap My Sovereign Sits."* [10]

Up-on my lap   my Sovereign

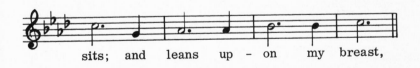

sits; and leans up - on my breast,

During this carol ARCHANGELS *come down, one from either side of the* CHORUS, *approaching the stable gently with folded hands. As carol ends, they open the doors*

and stand at either side before the CRÈCHE ANGELS.
MARY *is seen holding the child in her arms. Light from
him is shining on her face and enough auxiliary light
for a glow but not to take away the mystery.* MARY *sings
lullaby, unaccompanied—"Coventry Carol,"* [11] *refrain and
first verse only.*

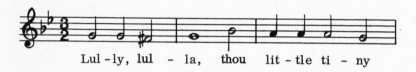

Lul-ly, lul - la, thou lit-tle ti - ny

Child, By by, lul - ly, lul - lay.

Toward the end of the carol, enter JOSEPH, *who pauses
when he sees the light. At the end of the lullaby, he
goes forward, kneels, and then enters the stable to stand
behind* MARY. COCK, RAVEN, OX, ASS, *and* LAMB *tiptoe
over to the stable, look at* MARY *and the baby, and
arrange themselves around the manger and stable as
the six* GREEN MEN OF THE WINTER SOLSTICE *enter dancing to the carol, "In Dulci Jubilo."* [12] *See the section on
the Dances. If the dance cannot be managed, enter two
mysterious* GREEN MEN *with green boughs, which they
wave rhythmically to music and make gifts of to
symbolize life everlasting. Lights come up very slowly.
Six* SHEPHERDS *enter reverently. A few at a time approach
the manger until all are there. It is still shadowy for it
is early dawn.)*

FIRST SHEPHERD: Is this the Messias?

SECOND SHEPHERD: Born in a stable?

THIRD SHEPHERD: 'Tis a shepherd, bethink thee. I have slept in a stable full oft.

FOURTH SHEPHERD: Yea, many a time I had not even a shed to cover me.

FIFTH SHEPHERD: And I, too.

FIRST SHEPHERD (*going up to manger*):   See He is a very child. How small He is!

(*Others all go up close and look.*)

SIXTH SHEPHERD: If this be the King, shall we not worship Him?

(SHEPHERDS *back away and kneel.*)

MARY: Rise, Herdsmen gentle, for now is He born, my darling dear One, to save all who love Him from harm. Draw nigh.

(*They approach one by one with gifts and return to places.*)

FIRST SHEPHERD (*kneeling at crèche*):   Hail, Blessed Lady! Hail, Son of Heaven! Take my poor greeting, this bob of cherries!

SECOND SHEPHERD: Lo! He smiles, my sweet One! Here is a bird to sing to Thee! Little Day Star!

FOURTH SHEPHERD: A ball do I bring. Here, stretch out Thy hand. Keep it and play with it withal. Thou art God, indeed!

THIRD SHEPHERD: Hail, Messias! Hail, lovely Babe! Share these, my last pennies.

FIFTH SHEPHERD: Cradle Thy head upon this little lamb, Thou Lamb of Heaven!

SIXTH SHEPHERD: Hail, Blessed Saviour! 'Tis but a sorry gift, this sprig of holly.

(SIXTH SHEPHERD *remains kneeling to the crèche while the following two lines of "The Holly and the Ivy"* [13] *are sung by a solo voice, a cappella:*

*"The holly bears a blossom as white as the lily flower,
And Mary bore sweet Jesus Christ to be our sweet Saviour."*

Enter CASPAR, BALTHASAR, MELCHIOR, *and* ATTENDANTS *to instrumental music or second verse of "Sing Aloud on This Day!"* [9] *Lights should be on fully by this time.*)

MELCHIOR: 'Tis the King of Kings whose star we have seen in the East!

CASPAR: Lo, how lowly He lies!

BALTHASAR: Here in a poor stable is born the great Prince, the Rose Isaiah, hath foretold.

(*First verse of "Lo, How a Rose"* [6] *is sung by* CHORUS *as* MELCHIOR *goes forward to make his gift at the manger.*)

MELCHIOR (*kneeling as his* ATTENDANT *hands him gift to place beside the manger*):
Gold for thy crown, great King of mighty kings!

(MELCHIOR *and* ATTENDANT *back away to take their*

places on the sides behind the SHEPHERDS. CASPAR *and*
BALTHASAR *and their* ATTENDANTS *do the same after
making their gifts.*)

CASPAR (*same action*):   Frankincense for Thine anointing,
O Messias!

BALTHASAR (*same*):   Bitter myrrh for the sorrow of the
world, O Saviour of mankind.

MARY (*rising with baby in arms*):
The Father of Heaven this night, God omnipotent,
That setteth all things aright, His son hath He sent.
And now is He born.
May He keep you from woe!
I shall pray Him do so.
Tell it forth as ye go!
And remember this morn.

(CHORUS OF ANGELS *sings triumphantly "Masters in This
Hall."* [14]

Mas-ters in this   hall,_Hear ye news to-day____

*Instruments, including hand-bells, can be employed to
great advantage. At the start of the third verse, the
lights begin to go down, and* SHEPHERDS *and* CASPAR,
BALTHASAR, *and* MELCHIOR *slowly drift off on both sides,
always keeping their eyes on the crèche. The scene is
the same as when the stable doors opened with* JOSEPH

and the OX, RAVEN, ASS, LAMB, *and* COCK. CHORUS
*leaves gradually. Those left sing until there are enough
outside to take up the song from a distance. The* ARCH-
ANGELS *slowly close the doors of the stable and stand
with folded hands. The only light is that of the star,
with a glimmer on the* CRÈCHE ANGELS. *As the last*
CHORUS ANGEL *leaves, the curtains close and the singing
dies away. If no curtains are used,* CHORUS *exits as it
entered, very quietly in the dark. For the ending, repeat
carols sung in the play, but quietly in the distance, like
an echo of what has gone before. "Tomorrow Shall Be
My Dancing Day"* [12] *or the "Sussex Carol"* [5] *might be
used.*)

In a Manger Laid

Cherry Tree Carol

Traditional Carol from Kentucky

On the sixth day of Jan-u-ary

His birth-day will be

When the star-s and the ele-ments

Shall trem-ble with glee

When the star-s and the ele-ments

Sha-ll trem-ble with glee.

In a Manger Laid

CAST OF CHARACTERS

FATHER, *who becomes* JOSEPH
MOTHER, *who becomes* MARY   FAMILY
JOHN, *who becomes a* SHEPHERD   *in the*
SARAH, *who becomes a worshiper at the crèche*   *play*
RUTH, *who becomes a worshiper at the crèche*

GABRIEL

CHERRY TREE

HEROD

QUEEN

HARPER *(a young boy)*   COURT

CUP BEARER   *for the Herod scene,*

CHIEF PRIESTS   *which may be omitted*

SCRIBES   *if a smaller cast*

ATTENDANTS   *is necessary*

SHEPHERDS *(ten or more)*

ANGELS OF THE CRÈCHE *(six)*

ARCHANGELS *(two older girls to open and close the*
                             stable doors)

OX

ASS

WISE MEN (*three*)

LARK ⎤

DOVE ⎟   *For the Dance of the Birds,*

RED BIRD ⎬   *which may be omitted if a smaller cast*

OWL ⎦   *is necessary*

CHORUS

ORCHESTRA

NOTE: The scene, the costumes for the family and corre-sponding characters in the play, and the carols are American, for Christmas is always contemporary and local. The words, except for the conversation of the family, which is con-temporary, have been selected from the King James Version of the Bible.

If it is preferred, the family need not become part of the play but may continue to sit in the room with the Father reading instead of Sarah. Other children take the parts in the play, and identification takes place through similar cos-tumes. Should more parts be needed, children may be added to the family and some speeches divided. Although not desirable, as it takes away from the intimacy, a group of nar-rators inconspicuously dressed may be seated off to the side of the stage opposite the family and do some of the reading.

FAMILY *enters, following* CHORUS *during singing of
"The First Noël," [1] and take places in front of curtain.
On an extension of the stage at one side is arranged a
comfortable room made effective by a rug, a few chairs,
a table on which there is a bowl of holly and books, and
a little Christmas tree. A cardboard backing can be
painted to complete a homelike scene. Furnishings must
be small.* CHORUS *sings first verse of "Wondrous Love." [15]*

What won-drous love is this, O my soul, O my

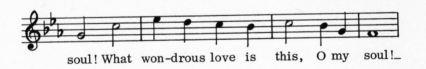

soul! What won-drous love is this, O my soul!_

Light comes up until there is good visibility on the
FAMILY.

FATHER: Tonight is Christmas Eve, when we celebrate
the birthday of the Christ Child. While we read the
story, as it is told in the Bible, imagine to yourselves
that it is taking place, not two thousand years ago in
the faraway Holy Land, but tonight on our farm here,
in these fields where you have walked, and that the

Baby Jesus was born in a red barn like ours. His mother will look to you like your mother.

MOTHER: If Jesus doesn't look to you like our baby, He won't seem real; but we keep on thinking about Him as the Son of God.

JOHN: I know the Christ Child is the Son of God, but I like to think of Him playing on our hills and of the shepherds looking after their sheep as we do in Cold Springs pasture.

SARAH: It would be funny, though, to see kings in our barn, or bright-robed angels there; it would be exciting, and I suppose that would be a miracle. I do wish it could all happen here tonight.

FATHER: Through our imagination it can, for that is how God speaks to us.

SARAH: Then you mean we can almost imagine the story is happening to us? How wonderful to think we could be really a part of it, not just listening!

FATHER: Yes, for if it's to mean anything real, we must think of the people we know and love best, yet more, of course, than everyday life.

MOTHER: Do you understand what Father means?

JOHN: I think so, us, but glorified.

MOTHER: Yes. Some of the Christmas carols that we love to sing, like the story, came long ago from across the sea but are at home here and belong to us now.

SARAH: Do you mean like "Jesus Born in Bethlea"?

MOTHER: That's one. I used to sing that to you when you were a baby.

(*The first line of "Jesus Born in Bethlea"* [16] *is sung by the* FAMILY. *The whole* CHORUS *picks up the rest of the first verse.*)

MOTHER: And now, Ruth, I wonder if you can remember some of the words of a prophecy of the coming of Christ?

RUTH: I think so— "Break forth into joy and sing together for all the ends of the earth shall see the salvation of our God. Ye shall go forth with joy and be led forth with peace; the mountains and the hills shall break forth before you into singing and all the trees of the fields shall clap their hands. Instead of the thorn shall come up the fir tree and it shall be to the Lord for an everlasting sign."

FATHER: Yes, our Christmas tree is a sign to us of everlasting life. (*Opening the Bible*) And here is the story of the birth of the Christ Child, according to the words of the Holy Gospel. (*Beginning to read*) "The word of God came unto John, The Baptist, preaching in the wilderness—" You know that part, John.

JOHN (*springs up. He has in hand a crook, the end of which he has been whittling*): Oh! Yes, I know that. "Prepare ye the way of the Lord, make his paths straight; every valley shall be filled and every hill shall be brought low and the crooked shall be made straight, and the rough ways shall be made smooth. He that hath two coats, let him impart to him who hath none; and him that hath meat, let him do likewise. One mightier than I cometh, the latchet of whose shoes I am not worthy to unloose. He shall baptise you with the Holy Ghost and with fire."

(CHORUS *sings the refrain only, "Come all ye out of the wilderness," from the "Seven Joys of Mary."* [17])

FATHER (*reading*):   Now the birth of Jesus Christ was on this wise.

(*Curtains open to width of one "flat" painted to represent a porch looking into an orchard.* MOTHER *goes over slowly to stand in front of this little scene. She has the sewing in her hand that she can slip unseen into her pocket. To the children she has become* MARY. FATHER *continues to read.*)

The angel Gabriel was sent from God unto a city of Galilee, named Nazareth, to a virgin espoused to a man whose name was Joseph, of the house of David; and the virgin's name was Mary. And the angel came in unto her.

(*Enter* GABRIEL *swiftly, as though appearing from heaven, with lily raised.*)

GABRIEL: Hail, thou that art highly favored, the Lord is with thee. Blessed art thou among women!

MARY: What manner of salutation may this be?

GABRIEL: Fear not, Mary, for thou hast found favor with God. And, behold, thou shalt bring forth a son and shalt call His name Jesus. He shall be great, and shall be called the Son of the Highest, and the Lord God shall give unto Him the throne of his father David. And

He shall reign over the house of Jacob forever; and of
His kingdom there shall be no end.

MARY: How shall this be?

GABRIEL: The Holy Ghost shall come upon thee, and the
power of the Highest shall overshadow thee. Therefore
also that holy thing which shall be born of thee shall
be called the Son of God.

(*Exit* GABRIEL.)

MARY (*sinks to knees facing front*):   My soul doth mag-
nify the Lord, and my spirit hath rejoiced in God my
Saviour. For He hath regarded the low estate of His
handmaiden. For, behold, from henceforth all generations shall call me blessed. For He that is mighty hath
done to me great things; and holy is His name. And
His mercy is on them that fear Him from generation to
generation. He hath showed strength with His arm; He
hath scattered the proud in the imagination of their
hearts. He hath put down the mighty from their seats
and exalted them of low degree. He hath filled the hun-
gry with good things; and the rich He hath sent empty
away. He hath holpen His servant Israel, in remembrance
of His mercy; as he spake to our fathers, to Abraham,
and to His seed forever.

(MARY *stands with back to audience, looking into
orchard.*)

FATHER: It came to pass in those days that there went out
a decree from Caesar Augustus that all the world should
be taxed, and all went to be taxed, every one into his
own city. Joseph also went up from Galilee, out of the

city of Nazareth, into Judaea, unto the city of David,
which is called Bethlehem (because he was of the house
and lineage of David) to be taxed with Mary, his espoused
wife, being great with child.

(FATHER *goes to join* MOTHER, *so becoming* JOSEPH *in the
eyes of the children watching.* CHORUS *sings all the verses
of "The Cherry Tree Carol,"* [18] *at the beginning of which
the* CHERRY TREE *enters and stands in front of the curtains
at the right.* MARY, JOSEPH, *and the* CHERRY TREE *dance in
pantomine. See the section on the Dances. Curtains close.*)

RUTH (*reading*):   While they were there, the days were
accomplished that she should be delivered. And she
brought forth her firstborn son, and wrapped Him in
swaddling clothes, and laid Him in a manger; because
there was no room for them in the inn.
Now when Jesus was born in Bethlehem of Judaea, it was
in the days of Herod the King.

(*The tune, "Soldier Boy," is played as an accompaniment
to the dance processional with which the* ATTENDANTS
enter from the left, in front of the curtains, HEROD *and
the young* QUEEN *leading. See the section on the Dances.
From the right, enter* HARPER, CUP BEARER, *and two* AT-
TENDANTS *carrying stool on which* QUEEN *may sit near*
HEROD. *Another two* ATTENDANTS *carry a rich hanging
suspended from a pole, to suggest a throne when* HEROD
stands before it with the CHIEF PRIESTS *and* SCRIBES *gathered around him. Wine is offered to* HEROD *who, after a
taste, hands it to the* QUEEN, *who sips it and hands it
back to* HEROD, *who quaffs it, drops a ring in the cup, and
returns it to* CUP BEARER. *This is merely "business" to*

suggest luxurious court and HEROD *in a happy mood in contrast to what follows.*)

HARPER (*sits on steps at feet of* HEROD *and chants a wedding hymn to* HEROD *and* QUEEN, *or recites it, as he seems to accompany himself on the American dulcimer or a small harp*):

I speak of the things which I have made touching the king; my tongue is the pen of a ready writer.

Gird thy sword upon thy thigh, O most mighty, with thy glory and thy majesty.

Upon thy right hand stands the queen in gold of Ophir. The king shall greatly desire thy beauty, for he is thy lord; and worship thou him.

I will make thy name to be remembered in all generations; therefore shall the people praise thee forever and ever.

(QUEEN *tosses him a flower.*)

RUTH: Behold, there came wise men from the East to Jerusalem.

(CHORUS *sings the first verse of* "The Babe of Bethlehem." [19]

Ye Na-tions all on ye I call, come

hear this dec - la - ra - tion

During the carol the WISE MEN *are ushered in from the left and are acknowledged by* HEROD, QUEEN, *and* ATTENDANTS. WISE MEN *bow and look around questioningly.*)

FIRST WISE MAN: Where is He that is born King of the Jews?

SECOND WISE MAN: For we have seen His star in the East and have come to worship Him.

(HEROD, QUEEN, *and* ATTENDANTS *show consternation.*)

RUTH: When Herod the King had heard these things, he was troubled, and all Jerusalem with him. He gathered all the chief priests and scribes of the people together and demanded . . .

HEROD: Where shall Christ be born?

CHIEF PRIEST (*fearfully reading from scroll*): In Bethlehem of Judaea. For thus it is written by the prophet: "And thou Bethlehem, in the land of Juda, art not the least among the princes of Juda, for out of thee shall come a Governor that shall rule my people Israel."

THIRD WISE MAN: Kings shall come to the brightness of His rising. The glory of the Lord is risen, and His glory shall be seen. The sun shall be no more thy light by day. Neither for brightness shall the moon give light unto thee. But the Lord shall be unto thee an everlasting light— and thy God thy glory.

HEROD (*dismisses* COURT, *who leave hastily, in dismay. Turns to* WISE MEN, *speaking craftily*): What time did the star appear? Go and search diligently for the young Child;

and when ye have found Him, bring me word again that
I may come and worship Him also.

(WISE MEN *bow and are ushered out through audience to
the second verse of accompaniment of the "The Babe of
Bethlehem."* [19] HEROD *watches them go as if they were his
doom. Lights go down except for spotlight on* HEROD.)

HEROD (*in despair*):
My days are consumed like smoke,
And my bones are burned as an hearth . . .
I am like a pelican of the wilderness;
I am like an owl of the desert.
I watch and am as a sparrow alone upon the housetop . . .
O my God, take me not away in the midst of my days.

(CHORUS *sings the fourth verse of "The Babe of Bethlehem,"* [19] *or orchestra plays the tune as* HEROD *exits. The
light of the star comes on.*)

RUTH: And there were in the same country shepherds
abiding in the field, keeping watch over their flock by
night.

(CHORUS *sings first verse of "My Shepherd Will Supply
My Need."* [20]

A group of SHEPHERDS *enter from the audience singing*

*unaccompanied except for the recorder that one is play-
ing.* JOHN *joins them. They stop on steps leading up to
the stage, singing and looking up at the star. As* RUTH
*begins to read again, the curtains are drawn wide for the
first time, showing the full radiance of the scene, one
of snowy hills. Lights are fully on. In the background are
painted clapboard houses, bare trees, a stone wall or rail
fence—anything to emphasize the American quality and
locale. In the center at the back stands a neat red barn,
with closed double doors two steps up. The entering*
SHEPHERDS *sink down among other* SHEPHERDS *who, already there, are kneeling with backs to the audience looking up at the* ANGELS *who on either side of the stable are
playing their instruments.*)

RUTH: And lo, the angel of the Lord came upon them, and
the glory of the Lord shone round about them, and they
were sore afraid.

ANGEL (*one of those of the crèche*): Fear not, for, behold, I
bring you good tidings of great joy, which shall be to all
people. For unto you is born this day in the city of David
a Saviour, which is Christ the Lord. And this shall be a
sign unto you: Ye shall find the Babe wrapped in swaddling clothes, lying in a manger. Glory to God in the
highest, and on earth peace, good will toward men.

(SHEPHERDS *slowly rise, looking up at* CHORUS *on either
side and listening in amazement. There is not much movement by the* SHEPHERDS, *but rather a picture of awe and*

wonder. Part of the CHORUS *sings verses of "Go Tell It on the Mountain."* [21] *The full* CHORUS *joins in refrain.)*

Go tell it on the moun-tain   O-ver the hills and

ev - 'ry - where!   Go   tell   it   on   the

moun - tain that   Je - sus Christ   is   born

FIRST SHEPHERD: Let us now go even unto Bethlehem and see this thing which is come to pass, which the Lord hath made known unto us.

(*The first verse of "My Shepherd Will Supply My Need"* [20] *is repeated as the lights begin to go down until there is only a glimmer on the* CRÈCHE ANGELS. *Instead of leaving, as they started to do, the* SHEPHERDS *look back at the* ANGELS *and decide to stay to see the wonders. They walk quietly to the far right and kneel in a group in the shadows while the* CHORUS *sings the first verse of "Wondrous Love."* [15]

As the carol begins, two ARCHANGELS *from the* CHORUS

*come down with folded hands and slowly open the doors
just as the carol is ending.* MARY *is sitting in the stable
with the baby in her arms or kneeling with the baby in
straw on the floor before her—in either case in such a
way that the light from the baby shines on her face.
There should also be faint auxiliary light so that the
stable can be seen faintly. Fresh straw is inside and a
well-filled manger by which the* OX *and* ASS *can be seen
kneeling.*

MARY *sings the first verse of "Jesus Born in Bethlea"* [16]
as an unaccompanied lullaby. As she is finishing, enter
JOSEPH *carrying a lantern. He stops and looks astonished.*
MARY *welcomes him. He hangs up the lantern, enters the
stable, and stands behind* MARY, *who sits on a stool holding the baby. Enter* RED BIRD, LARK, DOVE, *and* OWL *who,
after dancing around, settle by the crèche. For the dance
and the tune accompanying it, see the section on the
Dances.* SHEPHERDS *go over reverently to the stable to
look at* MARY *and the baby, then back away.*)

SECOND SHEPHERD: Oh come, let us worship and bow
down. Let us kneel before the Lord our Maker; for we
are the people of His pasture and the sheep of His hand.

(*All kneel except one or two who lean on crooks.*)

THIRD SHEPHERD: The Lord is my shepherd; I shall not
want.

FOURTH SHEPHERD: Thy rod and Thy staff, they comfort me.

FIFTH SHEPHERD: Surely goodness and mercy shall follow
me all the days of my life.

(*Some gifts are presented—a bird, a crook, a pipe—by* SHEPHERDS *who have no lines.*)

SIXTH SHEPHERD: The Dayspring from on high hath visited us, to give light to them that sit in darkness, to guide our feet unto the way of peace.

(*Lights slowly come up fully.* CHORUS *sings two verses of "Star in the East."* [22] WISE MEN *enter from audience. They stand on the steps leading to the stage, looking at the star for a moment; then go forward one by one to make their own gifts, even if they have* ATTENDANTS *who have carried them in.* WISE MEN *and* ATTENDANTS *back away from the stable and take positions in the group. This is all done during the carol and the next reading.*)

RUTH: And lo, the star which the Wise Men had seen in the East, went before them till it came and stood over where the young Child was. And when they saw the star, they rejoiced with exceeding great joy.

When the Wise Men were come into the house, they saw the young Child with Mary, His mother, and fell down and worshipped Him; and when they had opened their treasures, they presented unto Him gifts; gold, and frankincense, and myrrh.

(CHORUS *sings the refrain only of "Star in the East."* [22]

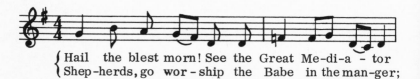

{ Hail   the blest morn! See the Great Me-di-a - tor
{ Shep-herds, go wor - ship the Babe   in the man-ger;

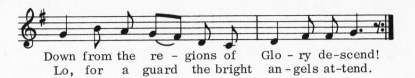

Down from the re - gions of   Glo - ry de-scend!
Lo,   for   a   guard the bright an - gels at-tend.

Chorus:

Bright - est and best of the   sons   of the morn-ing,

During the carol RUTH *and* SARAH *walk hand in hand to
the stable.* SARAH *sits with her head against* MARY'*s knee,
looking up into her face as* MARY *caresses her, making*
MARY *and* MOTHER *one.* JOSEPH *holds out his hand to* RUTH,
who steps into the stable by him.)

OLD SHEPHERD (*steps up to the stable, takes child in his arms,
goes a few steps downstage, and looks up as though
praying*): Lord, now lettest thou Thy servant depart in
peace, according to Thy word; for mine eyes have seen
Thy salvation, which Thou hast prepared before the face
of all people, a light to lighten the Gentiles, and the glory
of Thy people Israel.

(*Blesses the child and gives him back tenderly to* MARY,
who stands to receive him and remains standing.)

MARY:
My Son shall grow as the lily
And be as the dew
His branches shall spread
And His beauty shall be as the olive tree.

They that dwell under His shadow
Shall revive as the corn and grow as the vine
For this Child shall grow and wax strong in spirit
For the grace of God is upon Him.

(CHORUS *sings the "Ancient Moravian Christmas Carol."* [23]

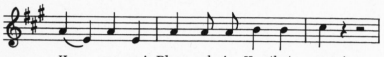

Ho - san-na! Bless-ed is He that comes!

At the end of the first verse, lights begin to dim slowly; MARY *sits quietly. Exit all, except* FAMILY *and the* OX *and* ASS *at the manger, one by one or few at a time from the side of the stage, backing away or looking back. The last to go are* RED BIRD, LARK, DOVE, *and* OWL. *Only* MARY, JOSEPH, *and the* OX *and* ASS *are left, and one shepherd boy* (JOHN) *kneeling. The stable is as it was when opened except for a dim spotlight for* JOHN.)

JOHN (*rises, looks into stable, and walks quietly into spot*):
In Him is life; and the life is the light of men. And the Light shineth in the darkness—the true Light which lighteth every man that cometh into the world. And the Word was made flesh and dwelt among us full of grace and truth.

(JOHN *kneels.* CHORUS *sings first verse of "Wondrous Love."* [15] *The stable is as it was when opened, with only the light of the baby on* MARY's *face and a very soft radiance in the barn. At the end of the first verse,* CHORUS *begins*

*to leave, softly singing various carols from the play.
When enough are outside to be heard, they sing again
verses of some of the carols until all are off.* ARCHANGELS
*close the doors and stand with their backs to them, hands
folded. The curtains close slowly.*

If the members of the FAMILY *do not take the parts of
the characters in the play, add the following ending.*)

FATHER (*closing the Bible*): This is the end of the Christmas story, or maybe it is just the beginning. And now it
is time to go to bed.

(*All exit quietly through the curtains as* CHORUS *sings
quietly in the distance "Jesus Born in Bethlea." [16]*)

Born in a Stable

The Truth from Above

Traditional Carol from England

This is the truth sent from a-bove,

The truth of God, the God of love,

There-fore don't turn me from your door,

But harken all- both rich and poor.

Born in a Stable

CAST OF CHARACTERS

Prologue

    MARY (*not the same as in the play*)

    JOSEPH (*not the same as in the play*)

The Play

    AUGUSTUS CAESAR

    HERALD

    MARY

    JOSEPH

    EZRA, *hard-hearted innkeeper*

    NAN, *keeper of another inn and owner of the stable*

    MAIDS

    SHOEMAKER ⎤

    WEAVER |

    CHRISTOPHER |

    ABIGAIL   ⎬   TAXPAYERS

    WILL |

    DICON |

    MARTHA |

    JAMES   ⎦

JUGGLERS, TUMBLERS, *and other* TAXPAYERS
   (*numbers to suit children available*)
OX
ASS
LAMB
ANGELS OF THE CRÈCHE (*six*)
GUARDING ANGEL
ARCHANGELS (*two older girls to open and close
   the stable doors*)
APPLE TREE
SHEPHERDS (*three*)
CASPAR, BALTHASAR, *and* MELCHIOR, *the Three Kings*
ATTENDANTS (*three*)
CHORUS (*older boys and girls*)
ORCHESTRA
HAND-BELL RINGERS (*if available*)

NOTE: AUGUSTUS CAESAR, HERALD, the GUARDING ANGEL, CASPAR,
   BALTHASAR, MELCHIOR, and the three ATTENDANTS may be
   omitted if a smaller cast is necessary.

PROLOGUE

CHORUS *sings first and last verses of "This Is the Truth Sent from Above"* [24] *before the curtains open. When the curtains are pulled part way,* MARY *and* JOSEPH *can be seen before a painted panel. They are dressed very differently from the two in the play so that it is understood this is introductory. There is a dance pantomime performed to "The Virgin Unspotted,"* [25] *collected and arranged by Cecil J. Sharp.*

The Vir - gin un - spot - ted, the

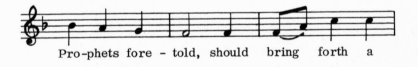

Pro-phets fore - told, should bring forth a

Sa - viour, which now you be - hold,

See the section on the Dances for directions. Curtains close.

69

THE PLAY

Before the curtain, on an elevation on one side of stage, enter AUGUSTUS CAESAR *and* HERALD.

AUGUSTUS:

My name Augustus Caesar is,
The entire world I wys
Is subject to my will.
No man may say aught is his
But by my leave be granted.
Therefore as lord I do declare
To prove my might and power
Each man shall one penny pay.
This is my will. Do as I say.
And by that penny, well is it spent,
Comes knowledge to be obedient.

(*Says to* HERALD *to whom he hands scroll*)

Warn them, boy, I command thee,
To everyone say this from me.
So all the world shall know that we
Are Sovereign of them all.

(*Exit* AUGUSTUS.)

HERALD (*walking to center of stage, unrolls scroll and calls to
    the audience*):
    Peace! I bid King and Knight,
    Men and women and each wight,
    'Til I have told you, and right
    Stand still, both stiff and stout.
    My lord Augustus, of great might
    Commands tribute of each one.
    A penny of each man wills he,
    'Til value of ten pence will be,
    To know that he has sovereignty
    Fully, of all mankind.

(*On the other side of stage from* AUGUSTUS CAESAR, MARY
and JOSEPH *enter, listening to* HERALD. *Behind them
gather the* SHOEMAKER *and* WEAVER *and some other people,
listening in dismay. People murmur.*)

SHOEMAKER:
    Oh, Lord! What does this man mean?
    I fear from this boaster here
    Tribute I must pay.

WEAVER:
    I've had little work for seven years.
    Now comes this King's messenger
    To get all that he may.

JOSEPH:
    With this awl and hammer here
    I have won my meat,
    As a simple carpenter
    Whatever I might get.

(*To* HERALD)

Please, sir, tell me, I thee pray.
Must poor as well as rich men pay?
My faith, sir, I hope, nay,
For that were monstrous wrong.

HERALD:

Good man I warn thee in good faith
To Bethlehem to take thy way.
Lest thou in danger fall today
If that thou be too long.

(*Exit with flourish. Dismay on part of people.*)

JOSEPH:

Now since it may no other be,
Mary, daughter, now go we.
All our silver will tribute be
For so we have been told.

(*More murmuring and talking as all exit toward back.*
CHORUS *sings two verses of "Christmas Eve."* [26])

SCENE: *Curtains (if used) open slowly to reveal Bethle-*
hem—the street of the inns. Lively instrumental music
such as "Greensleeves" [31] *accompanies the following pan-*
tomime. Violins and clarinet are nice. If scenery is used,
a little medieval village of crowded but attractive cot-
tages might be pictured, with two inns indicated by signs,
at either side, down front. In the center at the back is a
thatched barn, in bad repair. See the suggestions in the
section on Staging. The door is open and straw is on the

*floor. In the center is a manger full of hay, around which
sit an* OX, *an* ASS, *and a* LAMB. MAIDS *come out of the
inns, shake rugs, carry in jugs of water, etc., as if pre-
paring for guests.* EZRA *comes out of one inn, peers down
through the audience to see if any guests are coming, and
orders the* MAIDS *to hurry.* NAN *from the other inn goes to
the stable with a small basket of grain for the animals
and puts it in the manger. She strokes the* OX, ASS, *and*
LAMB, *they nuzzle her, and she goes back to her inn. So
Bethlehem, the inns, innkeepers, stable, and animals, all
so important to the play, are quickly established at the
beginning. The* TAXPAYERS *begin to arrive, entering from
the back through the audience, and come up several steps
to the stage. They come in various groups—families,
young couples, men together. The* TUMBLERS *come playing leapfrog or turning cartwheels; some come along
looking glum. They are carrying bundles and baskets;
one plays a recorder. There is pantomime as they go to
the inns and knock on the doors or call.* EZRA *and* NAN
*step outside and stay ready for the next comer. Some are
taken; some who are turned down go to the other inn.
Each time as they apply for lodging, the people obviously
pay before entering. In spite of the fact that some are
tired, there is a general air of gaiety, and it is evident
that the people are going to have a good time as well as
pay taxes. This pantomime must not take too long, but
there should be no feeling of rush or confusion. Precision
is essential in all pantomime. Each character is played as
an individual and acts with imagination. At intervals
laughter and singing are heard from the inns. This makes
clear the contrast that follows when* MARY *and* JOSEPH
are excluded. The number of people depends on the num-

ber in the group. As the last person is entering an inn,
JOSEPH *and* MARY *enter behind the other travelers, com-*
ing up the steps onto the center of the stage with their
backs to the audience. They look around them, then turn.
They are obviously very tired. JOSEPH *has one arm around*
MARY *and a staff in the other hand. She has a little bundle*
in one arm and leans against JOSEPH'S *shoulder.*

JOSEPH:
To Bethlehem at last we've come!

MARY:
Ah, Joseph, what may this mean?
Some men I saw glad and merry,
Some sighing and sorry.

JOSEPH:
Mary, daughter, indeed to say,
Lodging I hope to find, we may,
For great lords of fine array
Occupy this city.
I pray, Lord God, grant by Thy great might
Unto Thy simple servant here,
And little Mary, to Thee dear,
A lodging for this night.

(JOSEPH *goes over to the inn of* EZRA *and knocks with*
his staff. Enter EZRA.)

JOSEPH (*with dignity but timidity*):
Sir, in great need now are we,
As you, yourself, in truth may see,
For bed and a warm hostelry
For my sweet wife and me.

    She is so weak and all weary
    And fain would she rest.
    Gracious sir, for thy mercy
    You will be greatly blest.

EZRA:

    Here there is no rest or bed
    For poor folk such as ye.
    The rich may lodge well at this inn,
    But they pay plentifully.

    (*Exit* EZRA. JOSEPH *turns back dejectedly to* MARY.)

MARY:

    God will help us, full well you know.
    Therefore, Joseph, be of good cheer.

    (*Points to the other inn.* JOSEPH *straightens up, goes
    over, and knocks. Enter* NAN.)

JOSEPH:

    I pray good woman help our plight.
    Here in this town we are alone.
    Grant us a lodging for the night,
    For it is cold as stone.

MARY:

    We have sought both up and down
    Through diverse streets in this city,
    But no room anywhere have we found
    Or people who have pity.

NAN:

    So many people have come to town

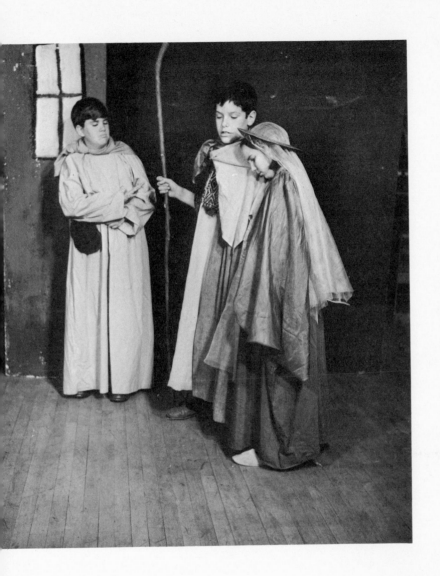

No more lodging here have we.
Indeed we are in such a press
I have no help for thee.

(*Seeing* MARY's *fatigue and* JOSEPH's *despair,* NAN *glances at the stable.*)

But in the stable with the beasts,
A poor room I confess.

(CHORUS *repeats the first verse of "This Is the Truth Sent from Above,"* [24] *which is sung as they go to look in the stable. The* OX, ASS, *and* LAMB *look up hopefully; they hang their heads as* JOSEPH *speaks.*)

JOSEPH:
And if we here all night abide
A storm may come upon the shed.
The walls are down on either side,
And roof lets rain in overhead.
Say, Mary daughter, what is thy will?
What shall we do?

(MARY *steps into the little shed, sits on a small stool behind the manger, and leans against some hay. The* LAMB *puts his head on her knee, and the* OX *and* ASS *come close.* NAN, *who started to be offended at* JOSEPH's *speech, smiles.*)

MARY:
It behooves us to bide here still,
For, sir, I think it is God's will.
The beasts are gentle. They'll keep me warm
And safe from harm.
Fain would I rest.

(*To* NAN)

For this stable tonight
May you be blest.

JOSEPH   (*to* MARY):
  Then I will get for you a light.
  It grows darker to my sight.
  And fuel bring to keep you warm
  Throughout this bitter night.

  (*To* NAN)

  Thank you, good woman, with you I'll go.
  I fear 'fore morning it may snow.

  (*He tucks* MARY's *cloak around her.* NAN *helps* JOSEPH *to close the stable doors.*)

NAN:
  Ah, Lord, but the weather is cold,
  The very worst freeze that ever I felt.

JOSEPH:
  Pray God, help me that am old,
  And little Mary, daughter, enfold,
  So I may say,
  Now, good God, my shield be
  As best you may.

  (*Exit* JOSEPH *and* NAN. GUARDING ANGEL *enters and stands on the steps in front of the stable doors with arms outstretched. There is the sound of music and laughter off stage, and out from the inns come people singing, dancing, and drinking.* EZRA *and* NAN *come out with large bowls of wassail. People dip in with their mugs, and*

*some drink and keep time while others dance to the
"Gloucestershire Wassail,"* [27] *verses one, two, three, seven,
and eight, sung by* CHORUS.

1. Was - sail, was - sail, all   o-ver the   town!__

*For the dance pantomime, see the section on the Dances.
Two or three boys do some tumbling and perhaps jug-
gling. Onlookers cheer and clap at success, jeer at mis-
takes. Enter a boy representing an* APPLE TREE, *who
stands in the center while all form circles around him,
dancing in a more ritualistic manner, as they sing. There
should be no breaks here. It all flows as an interlude of
jollity, whatever is done.* CHORUS *sings the "Apple Tree
Wassail"* [28] *from Somerset. See the section on the Dances
for directions. All exit to the inns dancing and singing
until song fades.*

*Lights go down except for a dim spotlight on a "hill"
off to the side of the stage. An Alleluia or a Gloria could
be sung here. Where* AUGUSTUS *stood, there now stands a
lone* SHEPHERD.)

SHEPHERD:

Now God in Trinity
Save my fellows and me.
I know not where my sheep may be.
The night is so cold;

It is near midnight.
Nowhere is there light.
I have no sight,
Standing alone on this dark hill.
I'll call with all my might.
My voice they know.
Ha-loo—Ha-low—
Ha-loo—Ha-low.

(*Two* SHEPHERDS *enter from the back or side of the audience.*)

SECOND SHEPHERD:
Hark! Hark! I hear our brother on the hill.

FIRST SHEPHERD:
Ha-loo—Ha-low—

SECOND SHEPHERD:
That is his voice I know.
Toward him let us go.
Follow his voice—Ha-loo—Ha-low—

FIRST SHEPHERD:
Ha-loo—Ha-low—

(*Calls back and forth to give a sense of distance and being lost.*)

THIRD SHEPHERD:
See, there he stands—
I'm right glad you are found.
Brother, where have you been so long?

FIRST SHEPHERD:
There came a gust of wind

That blew a mist so suddenly,
That off my way I went
And was full sore afraid.
I was so weary in this weather
As I wandered I knew not whither.

THIRD SHEPHERD:

Now, brother, you are passed your fright
And it be far into the night.
Here awhile let us rest.
Some cheese I have of the best.

(SHEPHERDS *eat, drink, and are merry. Suddenly one sees
the star in the sky.*)

SECOND SHEPHERD:

Brothers, look up and behold!
What thing is that shineth so bright?
As long as I have watched my fold,
I never saw such a sight.

(*All* SHEPHERDS *show wonder.* CHORUS *sings* "Hosanna." [29])

san - - - na!

Ho-san - - - na!

na! Ho - san - na!

ANGEL OF THE CRÈCHE:

Hear, courteous men,
This morn God's Son is born
In Bethlehem of a maiden free.

(CHORUS *sings one verse of "Ding-Dong! Merrily on High."* [30])

1. Ding dong! mer - ri - ly on

high In heav'n the bells are ring - ing;

FIRST SHEPHERD:

Hark! They sing above in the clouds!
Heard I never so merry a choir.

SECOND SHEPHERD:
> Now again I hear it come.

(CHORUS *sings second verse of "Ding-Dong!"* [30])

THIRD SHEPHERD:
> Mirth and comfort has come us among,
> For this is the sweetest of all songs.
> God's Son is come!

FIRST SHEPHERD:
> Glory! Glory! In Excelsis!
> It was their song.

SECOND SHEPHERD:
> Now go we hence
> To worship that Child
> And sing in His presence.

THIRD SHEPHERD:
> Now would I give both hat and horn that noble Child to see.

(*Exit* SHEPHERDS *as* CHORUS *sings refrain of "Ding-Dong!"* [30])

GUARDING ANGEL (*standing at closed stable door*):
> He came all so still to His mother's bower
> As dew in April that falls on the flower.
>
> He came all so still where His mother lay
> As dew in April that falls on the spray.
>
> Mother and maiden was never none but she,
> Well may such a lady God's mother be.

(*Lights go slowly down so that it is dark.* CHORUS *sings "There Is No Rose."* [31] *During the second verse,* ARCHANGELS *walk down with folded hands to the stable doors, which* they open just as carol ends. There must be no hurry; music may be repeated if necessary. The GUARDING ANGEL steps to one side, then kneels at the corner of the stable. The ARCHANGELS stand at either side of the stable with hands folded. MARY is seen, the baby in her arms, with the light of the baby shining on her face. There is a little auxiliary light (Christmas tree bulb), enough to enable the audience to see but not enough to take away from the mystery. The OX, ASS, and LAMB can just be seen kneeling and looking up at MARY and the baby. MARY, unaccompanied, sings gently several times to the baby the refrain of "Lullay My Liking" [32] or one verse of the Hebridean "Christ Child's Lullaby" [33] as below.)

My love, my pride, my treas - ure, O, my
won - der new, my pleas - ure, O, my

JOSEPH (*enters carrying lantern and wood and hurries toward stable. Stops when he sees doors open and a light within. Goes forward slowly.*):
Ah Lord God, what light is this
That comes shining so suddenly?
Say, Mary, daughter, what cheer with thee?

MARY:

> Right good, Joseph, as you may see.

JOSEPH (*still amazed—holding up lantern as he stands out-side at corner of shed*):

> Oh, Mary, what sweet thing is that on thy knee?

MARY:

> It is my Son, the truth to say, that is so young.

JOSEPH:

> I marvel greatly at this light,
> So shining is a wondrous sight.

(JOSEPH *kneels and worships.*)

> Now welcome, flower, fairest of hue,
> Hail, my Maker, hail Christ Jesu,
> Hail, my Lord, bringer of light.
> I shall serve Thee with main and might.
> Hail, blessed flower.

(JOSEPH *hangs up lantern, enters the stable, and stands behind* MARY, *looking at the baby—the "Holy Family" picture. Light has slowly come up a bit.*)

MARY:

> Now, Lord, that all the world shall win,
> Yet art my son, to Thee I pray.
> Here in this manger I might Thee lay
> Between these beasties three,
> All lapped about with straw,
> And I shall wrap Thee, my own dear child,
> With such things as we have.

(*Takes the veil from her head, wraps it around the baby,*

and lays him lovingly in the manger. ASS, OX, *and* LAMB
*come close to worship and keep the baby warm. Mean-
while,* SHEPHERDS *are entering.* CHORUS *sings one verse of
"Lullay My Liking."* [32])

FIRST SHEPHERD:
Brothers, here in the stable He doth lie.

SECOND SHEPHERD:
Now let us do Him homage.

THIRD SHEPHERD:
Who shall go first to make his gift?
(*To* FIRST SHEPHERD) You?

FIRST SHEPHERD (*to* THIRD SHEPHERD):
Nay, you be the furtherest in age.
Therefore you must first offer.

THIRD SHEPHERD (*going up to manger*):
Though I am but a simple knave,
Yet still I come of courteous kin.
Lo, here's such harness as I have,
A broach with bell of tin.

SECOND SHEPHERD:
I am too poor to make a present,
As my heart would, and I had aught.
Two cobble-nuts upon a band—
Lo! Little Babe, what I have brought.

FIRST SHEPHERD:
I have no present that you may please,
But a horn spoon I made here,
And it will hold good forty pease.

That will I give you with good cheer.
Such a spoon may not displease.
Farewell, thou little swain.

(SHEPHERDS *go to one side together, kneel, and watch all that happens.*)

JOSEPH:

O, Mary, behold these beasts so mild,
As loving in their manner as men.
Indeed it seems such is their care
That they their Lord do ken.

MARY:

Their Lord they know, that know I well.
They worship Him with might and main.
The weather is cold as you can tell.
They keep Him warm with their sweet breath.
Now sleeps my son. Blest may He be
And lies full warm the beasts between.

(MARY *puts her arms around the* OX, ASS, *and* LAMB, *and all worship the baby.*)

JOSEPH:

O, now is fulfilled, in truth I see,
The very ancient prophecy
That says, our Saviour shall be seen
Between the beasts to lie.

(CHORUS *sings the fourth verse of "Lullay My Liking."* [32] *Except for* JAMES, *any of the following speeches of the people may be omitted.*

During the carol, enter TAXPAYERS *from inns, quietly, in small groups. They listen to the carol—see the star. All go to look in the manger, then back away, sinking on their knees in a position (places carefully given) to make a picture, with* MARY *as the apex, of a triangle of which the audience forms the opposite long side and the people on the stage the two sides.)*

NAN (*who has been standing outside her door since the angel song, in amazement, with clasped hands*):
Take off your hat
The first as goes
To welcome the holy stranger.

(*All the people are on stage by now and kneeling, except for* CHRISTOPHER *and* ABIGAIL, *who stay by the manger. He stands—she sits.*)

CHRISTOPHER (*takes his sheepskin coat from his shoulders and lays it over corner of the manger*):
Little Jesus, sweetly sleep, do not stir;
We will lend a coat of fur.
See the fur to keep you warm,
Snugly round your tiny form.

ABIGAIL (*puts out a hand as though the manger were a cradle*):
Mary's little baby, sleep, sweetly sleep,
Sleep in comfort, slumber deep.
We will rock you, rock you, rock you.
We will serve you all we can,
Darling, darling little man.

(CHRISTOPHER *and* ABIGAIL *take their places in the group.*)

WILL (*a small child himself, standing up to peep toward the manger*):
Thou art so little to be King.

DICON (*going to stable, kneeling, and holding out whistle*):
I have brought a whistle, made of clean straight willow.

(*Other gifts, if desired, might be a crock of butter, a baby calf—anything homely.*)

MARTHA:
Little man, and God indeed,
Little and poor, Thou art all we need.
We will follow where Thou dost lead,
And we will heed our Brother, born of Mary.

JAMES (*a carpenter with a hammer and plank of wood in his hand, standing*):
I think this Child will come to be
Some sort of workman such as we,
So He shall have my tools and chattels,
My well-set saw, my plane, my drill,
My hammer that so merry rattles,
And planks of wood,
And planks of wood to work at will.

(*Puts hammer and wood by the manger. As* CHORUS *sings* "Somerset Carol" [34] *or the* ORCHESTRA *plays some instrumental music,* CASPAR, BALTHASAR, *and* MELCHIOR *enter through the audience. They pause on the steps to look at the star. All on the stage look at them, astonished. They may have* ATTENDANTS *who carry gifts, but* CASPAR, BALTHASAR, *and* MELCHIOR *make their own gifts at the manger as they make obeisance.*)

CASPAR:

    Hail, Lord, that all the world hath wrought,
    Hail, God and Man together here.
    A cup of gold I have Thee brought,
    In token that Thou hast no peer.

BALTHASAR:

    Hail, Lord from high heaven sent,
    In token of Thy priesthood, see,
    I bring a cup of frankincense
    To waft our prayers from man to Thee.

MELCHIOR:

    Hail, Saviour, Who for love of man
    Will suffer death upon the tree.
    This bitter myrrh a token then
    How dear is immortality.

    (KINGS *and* ATTENDANTS *take their place on the stage beyond the people.*)

AUGUSTUS CAESAR (*who has entered and watched*):

    Ah! This is a wondrous sight,
    For yonder I see a maiden bright,
    A young child in her arms alight,
    A bright cross on his head.
    Honor I will that sweet wight
    For this reverence is most right.

    (*Takes off crown and lays it by manger.*)

JAMES (*who has remained near the manger after making his gift speaks, as though in protection against the speech of* MELCHIOR):

Now golden-headed Mary, maid,
Take comfort and God speed ye.
We'll take our leave but don't be 'fraid
We'll never see ye needy.

MARY (*who took the baby on her lap at the approach of the
three* KINGS, *now stands with him in her arms. She speaks
slowly*):
Sing, heaven imperial, of all most high!
Regions of air make harmony;
Fish in water, fowls that fly
Be mirthful and make melody.
All Gloria in Excelsis cry!
Heaven, earth, sea, man, bird, and beast
He that is crowned above the sky,
For us, my son, born like the least.

(CHORUS *sings verses four, five, and six of the "Sussex
Mummers' Carol."* [35] *If necessary repeat verse six.*

Oh   mor - tal   man   re -

mem-ber well where   Christ   our Lord   was   born

During the second verse, the SHEPHERDS *come down
through the audience, pointing to the star as though*

*they were singing and praising God and telling all that
they had seen and heard. At the third verse the lights
begin to go down slowly, and those on the stage "drift"
off quietly on the two sides, always with their eyes on the
vision of the manger. At last the scene is as it was at the
opening of the stable doors—the only light glimmering
on the* CRÈCHE ANGELS. CHORUS *repeats two verses of
"This Is the Truth Sent from Above."* [24] *If necessary, this
can be followed by any verses from any carols—sung
softly. Just before the singing ends, the* ARCHANGELS *close
the doors slowly and stand with their hands folded. The
curtains close when all the* CHORUS *is off stage. If there are no
curtains, the stage is entirely dark while* CHORUS *and then*
ARCHANGELS *leave. This ending is quiet and lovely, but if
too long, it can make the ending flat—an anticlimax.)*

Suggestions for Production

PRODUCTION

Simplicity is the watchword. Any temptation that may be felt to "gild the lily" is unwisdom. The opportunity is rare to bring out the direct beauty of these old mystery plays through the direct unself-consciousness of children, but simplicity demands care in detail, for there is no concealment.

The director will, of course, give each person working on an aspect of the production a copy of the play and have a meeting at which plans are made, questions asked, a common view adopted, and responsibilities clearly assigned. Then the director will keep on coordinating until the play is given. There will be an infinite number of details to check on, draw together, and adjust, such as the costumes, properties, lighting, scenery, music, etc.

All decisions and changes must flow through the hands of the director if there is to be coherence.

We have found it useful to have a tape recording of the music to use in rehearsals, so that the timing can be allowed for. Then chorus and cast need to have only three or, at most, four rehearsals together.

HINTS FOR DIRECTING

THE PRELIMINARIES

These suggestions are for those who may not have worked with children on plays such as these.

1. Talk to the players about the play, where it came from, etc., so that it will have importance for them and they can see it as a responsibility and an opportunity to do something lovely and do it well.

2. Read the play as it should be given. (This means the director will have to be very familiar with it.)

3. Encourage questions. One that is sure to come up is why a light within a rubber doll, wrapped in cheesecloth, is used for the baby instead of merely a doll. Explain that a light is used because it is a symbol. (I am careful that they never see the light and doll until they are together and arranged in swaddling clothes—to preserve some mystery.)

4. Give a copy of the play to each one trying out and allow time to read it over—then and there. (Do not permit the children to take the copies home.) Tryouts for parts usually take considerable time but are worth it to directors, and all feel it is fair.

5. When, later, parts are announced, emphasize the importance of each one and its contribution to the whole that makes the play. These are not plays for stars. One careless person standing at the back can act as a smudge on a painting. The director must mean this and keep emphasizing the point all through the rehearsals. It is better to say everyone is a star.

6. Give out the play, and then the director should read it through again with the children following in their copies.

7. The children immediately thereafter read the play through,

each one reading his own part. Give some correction. Have them stand up in groups for this, with some approximation of the stage. Emphasize character ("What is he or she like?"), meaning, and clear, well-phrased speech from the beginning.

8. Tell the children to imagine who they are before learning the words. Talk a little about this—give examples, explain that they always have to think before speaking as in real life and then it will sound real, not rattled off. The same is true about gestures. Refer to a favorite TV star and tell them to notice these things.

9. NOTE: These preliminaries take time but are very important since children tend to revert in the actual play to what they did in the very beginning. All rehearsing is an extension and emphasis of the start. That is why, contrary to general practice, they should not learn their lines before they have the feel of their parts. Learning words is almost too easy for children, so let that follow imaginative understanding.

THE REHEARSING

1. The aim is to bring the parts into a coherent whole that moves toward a goal or conclusion. With this in mind, the director should do as little "directing" as possible—only bring out natural qualities with points of emphasis in timing, speaking, and grouping.

2. Have properties from the beginning so that the children can learn to handle them easily. Their use affects timing.

3. Have the children move naturally, take the stage when necessary, not sidle or back up, yet not overdo, as groupings tend to melt into one another. As grouping is important, get them to understand they must be placed thus and so, as a part of a whole, instead of mechanical "blocking." Have them watch from the back of the room. Break up large groups. The effect should be plastic, *not static*.

4. Emphasize, and never give up on, *clear, intelligent speech with good phrasing and suitable dramatic delivery*. Words need to be

spoken more slowly than they can imagine. It helps to have one of
them always at the back of the room. He usually says, "Can't hear,
louder!" Let those children with difficulty go to the back and listen. They will be surprised and impressed, and it usually helps.
Don't speak to the children of rhythm, but the director knows that
it is there and must come through.

5. Gestures are definite, simple, direct, and big—from the shoulder, not the wrist or elbow.

6. It has been helpful and has saved time and confusion to work
quietly with small groups, i.e., the KINGS, the SHEPHERDS, the
PROPHETS, JOSEPH and MARY, etc.

7. The director will, of course, have in mind what he wants
brought out in the play and point the action in that direction.

8. Along with respect for the children and love of the material,
the religious feeling, which is basic, will permeate the whole, but it
will be natural and simple, mixed with merriment, not sentimentality.

CHORUS

Contributed by Newell Price and Elsie Archer

As in the case of the cast, careful preliminary work needs to be done with the chorus before rehearsals begin. They, too, should have the play read to them and be told of its value and dignity and of the fact that they are an integral part of the play. Carrying the very beautiful music, as they do, is a responsibility and opportunity for each one to learn every word and sing his best. The grown people involved will have a common understanding beforehand as to what is expected and set the standards. The chorus can make or mar the whole effect.

We stress the discipline, for without it this kind of performance cannot succeed and so will leave a feeling of dissatisfaction with the children. If the chorus is large and the children are of different ages, this is a challenge but can be met by building pride.

At a school, the carols will be learned in small groups in classes; at a church or in a club, there will be different problems. The smaller the groups in the beginning, however, the better will be the result. When they all come together, the situation should be treated quite formally, and by then they should know their words and tunes. There should be a rehearsal without singing when places are assigned and they line up and learn to go in and out quietly, with no talking. Then there should be at least one rehearsal in their places, singing, before they are put together with the cast. A good plan is to have one rehearsal where the chorus may watch the play so that they can see how the carols fit and have a clear understanding of the whole. If the singing and attention are good, the director should say so.

The people in charge of the chorus need to be experienced. The arrangements, the morale, the dressing, and the getting them in and out are as important as are the detailed plans for the cast.

The girls sit with hands together, fingers below chins, elbows in. The boys sit grasping their gold spears with crosses on the top, shoulder high when seated.

There is no wriggling or moving. The beauty of the picture is a satisfaction and delight to children and audience alike.

MUSIC

Contributed by John Langstaff

Traditional folk carols are the basis of the music that forms an integral part of these plays, for, being similar in quality, they intensify the drama. The beauty of the melodic line and the variety of modes are fresh and natural. Their emotional gamut ranges from the tenderness of a lullaby to exaltation, mystery, ritual, and humor.

To provide music for the American play was a challenge, but fortunately there have been fine collectors of traditional music such as Cecil J. Sharp, John Powell, and John Pullen Jackson, who have found in this country American variants of English carols. Filtered by means of the oral tradition through the lives of the people here for two or three hundred years, they have acquired an unmistakably American idiom in thought, speech, and music. In the same way, many Negro songs have become traditional. Some music has been selected from Colonial and contemporary composers, but everything has been chosen with great care for its distinction, suitability for children, and relation to the play. In the two miracle plays, songs have been included that were sung between the fourteenth and seventeenth centuries. There is a wealth of early music and poetry available from medieval and Elizabethan sources.

The music is always sung from memory, often in unison by all of the children regardless of voice, but some songs have been set well for part-singing. Some gain by being sung *a cappella;* others are enhanced when sung by a small group of especially good singers. Occasionally a solo voice can take a line; but there is only one solo carol, the lullaby, sung unaccompanied, by the Virgin to her baby. Strings, woodwinds, hand-bells, percussion, and brass instruments can make a fine addition to the piano, but discretion is needed that young voices may not be lost. Instrumental music greatly enlivens processions, entrances, and exits of groups. Occasionally small fragments of carols, perhaps only a line, can be used as a musical "pointing-up," but this must be done with care not to interrupt the flow of the play. Such cues have to be fitted in smoothly and quickly and should be dispensed with if they can't be handled easily.

For those who may have few resources to turn to, we suggest *The Oxford Book of Carols* as invaluable and basic. Others will enjoy delving into a wide range of sources now available in libraries and music centers. A list of outstanding collections is given in the Appendix. The familiar Christmas hymns have not been used, as most of them do not suit the quality of the plays.

One word about teaching the music to children. Clear, unforced tone, good phrasing, and distinct enunciation are to be stressed in the singing. It is important to start work soon enough so that the rich vein of extraordinary tune, strong rhythm, and beautiful poetry that runs through so much of this music may be thoroughly comprehended. Many of the unfamiliar carols can be learned and sung at any season of the year. If the jubilation, mystery, and serenity of these carols infect the young singers, the chorus will add its own dramatic intensity to the play.

DANCES

Contributed by May Gadd,
Director of the Country Dance Society of America

All of the dances used in the plays are based on American or English folk forms, to fit the carols that they accompany.

In accordance with tradition, the steps used are natural—running, walking, or skipping—while the simple patterns are the basic ones of circles, arches, lines. The dance to the carol, "Tomorrow Shall Be My Dancing Day" or "In Dulci Jubilo," is done by boys and based on steps used in men's ritual Morris dances.

The dances are all a part of the action of the play and, in some cases, as in the Annunciation carol, are confined to rhythmic, unstylized movements, depicting the narrative that is being told by the singers.

This type of dancing is used because it is a part of the tradition and evolution of the mystery plays and the carols, and so helps to bring about unity of action, music, and song.

The dances given here are intended as suggestions. Some may want to follow them exactly as outlined; others may wish to devise other uses of the folk pattern and steps, according to their own experience or the number of children involved. In any case, it is recommended that simplicity and the traditional forms be retained, in order to keep the dances an integral part of the whole.

OLD CHRISTMAS

Pantomime of the Annunciation to the carol, "Nova, Nova," sung
by CHORUS or played by instruments
Characters: MARY, ANGEL GABRIEL

Verse 1. The curtains part slightly to show MARY sitting reading a book.

Verse 2. GABRIEL enters and bows to MARY, while she looks up from her book.

Refrain. GABRIEL turns around with a triumphant movement.

Verse 3. MARY kneels to GABRIEL.

Refrain. GABRIEL blesses MARY with his lily, moving around her gently.

Verse 4. MARY folds her hands across her breast to indicate submission.

Refrain. MARY and GABRIEL turn around with arms up high as the curtains close.

Dance of the GREEN MEN OF THE WINTER SOLSTICE to the carol, "In Dulci Jubilo," sung or played

Characters: six GREEN MEN OF THE WINTER SOLSTICE

Boys enter from the back of the hall, through the audience, to either the single or the double Morris step. The single Morris step consists of hop-right, hop-left (to each bar). The double Morris step, which is more difficult, consists of right, left, right, hop-right (to bar 1); then left, right, left, hop-left (to bar 2). The arms are swung down and up during each bar.

Verse 1. The first pair starts forward during the first half of the verse. The second pair begins to advance during the second half of the verse. The third pair begins to advance during the refrain.

Verse 2. The first pair dances up the steps and around the stage, ending facing the manger to dance the "obeisance."

Refrain. Bow to manger by springing onto left foot, with right leg stretched back on toe. Left knee is well bent, body is inclined forward, and arms are stretched out to the sides. Return to upright position, bringing the feet together, and conclude with two low jumps with feet together.

During the refrain the second pair has danced up the steps.

Verse 3 and refrain. As in verse 2 but with four boys dancing around in a circle and facing the manger in a semicircle for the refrain.

During the refrain the third pair has danced up the steps.

Verse 4 and refrain. As in verse 3 but with six boys dancing.

At the end of the dance, all walk to their appointed places by the manger.

An alternate carol for the dance of the GREEN MEN OF THE WINTER SOLSTICE is "Tomorrow Shall Be My Dancing Day."

The dance is essentially the same as for "In Dulci Jubilo," fitting the steps to the music. For the refrain, the dance movements must be repeated. This version is not advised for inexperienced dancers.

IN A MANGER LAID

Pantomime of the Annunciation to "The Cherry Tree Carol," sung by CHORUS

Characters: MARY, JOSEPH, and CHERRY TREE

MARY and JOSEPH are already in scene. Enter CHERRY TREE from the right. They depict the action of the carol in rhythmic pantomime, not too exactly, but indicate the story of the carol.

Processional entrance of COURT to the tune of "Soldier Boy," played on violin, clarinet, or piano

Characters: HEROD, QUEEN, CHIEF PRIESTS, SCRIBES, and ATTENDANTS

Partners, standing side by side, join right hands, lead forward (4 steps), and turn halfway to change places (4 steps). Do not drop hands. Continue to lead forward and turn, repeating as many times as needed.

Variant of Appalachian folk tune as used by Philip Merrill

Dance of the Birds to "Charlie's Sweet," played by ORCHESTRA or piano
Characters: LARK, DOVE, RED BIRD, and OWL

LARK enters from right to center and waves wings. DOVE enters
from left, and both dance around. RED BIRD enters from right,
and all dance to the manger and wave wings as if bowing.
All flutter around the stage in different directions. All dance
around clockwise and wave wings. All meet in center and then
turn away. RED BIRD dances to the manger and sits. DOVE and
LARK dance to the manger and sit. OWL prances out to center
and faces front. OWL turns head to right, to left, to front, and
nods twice. OWL revolves slowly. OWL then prances to the man-

ger and sits close to MARY, and all nod.

STEPS: All except OWL use skipping step. OWL mainly "prances."

Variant of Appalachian folk tune as used by Philip Merrill

BORN IN A STABLE

Introductory pantomime to "The Virgin Unspotted," sung by CHORUS

Characters: JOSEPH and MARY

A gentle waltz step is used for this dance.

Verse 1. Enter stage right, cross to the left to look at the inn, cross to the right to look at the other inn, and then move to the center of the stage.

Refrain. Turn around with right hands joined.

Verse 2. JOSEPH pivots, bringing MARY around him. He then passes behind her, holding out his cloak, while she bends as if putting her baby down.

Refrain. Both circle around the baby, looking down.

Verse 3. Both waltz around stage, JOSEPH protecting MARY with his cloak.

Refrain. At the stage left, turn with right hands and exit during the last line.

Pantomime to the "Gloucestershire Wassail," sung by CHORUS and by dancers informally

Characters: HORSE and COW (two of the TAXPAYERS), BUTLER (EZRA with bowl), MAIDS (with lily-white smocks), and TAXPAYERS to make three to five dancing couples. HORSE and COW should not be realistic but can put on something to indicate their characters, e.g., a gray kerchief for the HORSE, a red one for the COW.

A hearty, informal skipping step is used for this dance.

Verse 1, first half. HORSE and COW enter skipping and acting parts sufficiently to indicate character. MAIDS and TAXPAYERS follow, waving drinking cups. HORSE and COW skip around and off to the back of the stage.

Verse 1, second half. Couples dance on with partners, half from the inns at each side, turn partners with the right hand, and end in a ring.

Verse 2. HORSE dances into the middle of the ring and gallops around, while ring circles left (eight steps) and right (eight steps).

Verse 3. Boy and girl nearest the back make an arch; HORSE exits to the back through the arch, while boy and girl nearest to the front separate and lead the others behind the arch and under it to the front, following the COW, who comes under the arch first. The "cast-off" can be repeated, the COW leading the left-hand file, again coming through the arch and going off to the back. The dancers end in original circle.

Verse 4. BUTLER comes into the middle while dancers circle left (eight steps). They then close in on the BUTLER (four steps), girls fall back (four steps), while boys join hands to make high arches, taking a step back to make as big a circle as possible.

Verse 5. Girls dance in and out under the arches. They end in any place because, as this circle ends, TUMBLERS and JUGGLERS skip from spectators to front. They tumble, with dancers applauding, jeering, clapping, until the "Apple Tree Wassail" begins.

Ceremonial dance to "Apple Tree Wassail"[28] (Somerset), sung by CHORUS and by dancers informally

Characters: APPLE TREE, TAXPAYERS, and MAIDS

There should be a ceremonial feeling to the dance.

APPLE TREE enters and takes center position, while dancers circle around him clockwise with sixteen rhythmic walking steps. "To blow well . . . "—dancers stand in a ring with hands joined and they swing arms up and down.

At the end they all shout, "Caps full!" "Hats full!" "Barns full!" etc., while picking up paper apples and throwing them to the audience. APPLE TREE exits, and others go off, singing informally, to the inns, until tune dies in the distance.

Allegretto

Old ap - ple tree_ we'll was-sail thee,_ And

hop-ing thou wilt bear_ The Lord does know_where

we shall be To be mer - ry an - oth - er

year_ To_ blow well and to bear well And so

mer-ry let us be___ Let ev - 'ry man_ drink

1st time.

up his cup_ And health to the old ap -ple

2nd time.

tree._ To_ health to the old ap -ple tree._

COSTUMES

Contributed by Helen Fox
Assisted by Faith Marr

Costumes should be as simple as possible, but great care should be taken that folds are graceful and colors beautiful and harmonious when they are grouped on the stage. Sometimes a costume that in itself is good will clash with others near it and have to be changed. Line and color are of the utmost importance. When dressing the children, care is taken that safety pins, those stand-bys and necessities, do not show, that raw edges are tucked in, ravelings cut off, and belts, kerchiefs, and headdresses well adjusted. The general appearance depends on the care in detail, which people who are inexperienced in giving plays with children may easily overlook or take for granted.

The costumes for *Old Christmas* and *Born in a Stable* are of the fourteenth or fifteenth centuries. The colors are soft, rich, plain. The costumes for *In a Manger Laid* are approximately of 1900, although it does not have to be exact. Costumes and scene in this play are of a time of farm life and family comfort that make Americans nostalgic.

The detailed account of costumes that follows should be considered a guide, suggestions to give help, not a must. It is fun to get books from the library, go to museums, collect old Christmas cards, and evolve your own. Only remember that two of the plays are pre-Renaissance and so the costumes are simple. Costumes in the Herod scene in the American play may be made either Palestinian or medieval. Children may enjoy doing research and designing, but adult supervision will be necessary to keep the costumes suitable and practical.

OLD CHRISTMAS

The Prophecy

PEOPLE and PROPHETS in long robes, PEOPLE in somber colors, the PROPHETS in soft colors.

CRÈCHE ANGELS: Tunics of double cheesecloth with a hole cut in the center for the head, sewed at sides, hand dyed, two each of soft shades of lavender, pink, yellow. Should be made very long to cover the feet when sitting on the "perch" by the stable and full enough to hang gracefully. Neckerchiefs to match costumes; tiny wings of buckram with cotton glued on and a touch of glitter—points just peep over the shoulder; a halo made of buckram sprayed with gold.

In the dance pantomime to the Annunciation carol—

MARY: Blue dress, soft enough to fall in full and graceful folds—rather like a Botticelli Madonna; no veil but a halo.

GABRIEL: Red and gold robe, floor length; large wings of buckram over wire, painted to represent feathers in red and gold; sandals painted red or gold; a halo.

The Fulfillment

JOSEPH: Simple long robe, neutral or soft green; a soft brown hood pushed down around the neck; nothing on head. A brown sleeveless cloak open in front with a few pleats at back and in front to make it fall well is especially good and should be used in *Born in a Stable,* where Joseph walks around with his back to the audience.

MARY: Simple deep rose-colored dress, full enough to be graceful, with flowing sleeves of filmy blue material or a floating blue outer robe; filmy white veil (in *Born in a Stable* it should be long in back) not too much over the head or made to look like a nun's headdress; a halo.

SHEPHERDS: Tunics are made of outing flannel, hand dyed in soft earth tones, brown, orange, rose, green, blue, yellow, etc. They may be made from one piece of material with a hole cut for the head. Little if any sewing at the sides is necessary unless no belt is used. Length of tunics can be varied. Ties for the waists, headpieces, and neckerchiefs can be made from the dyed materials—often in contrasting colors to the tunic. Headdresses are put on in different ways and often allowed to fall around the shoulders or down the back. Don't smother the children with material. The boys wear long khaki pants, laced to the knees with narrow strips of fabric, or colored tights. The girls wear different-colored tights. Long-sleeved sweaters can be worn under the tunics to cover the arms. The girls wear suede dancing sandals, which can be dyed.

COCK, RAVEN, OX, ASS, LAMB : Headdresses: tight-fitting hoods made of fabric so as to suggest the animal by color and characteristic touch—i.e., red coxcomb for COCK, yellow bill for RAVEN, large ears for ASS, horns for OX, little ears for LAMB. Faces are uncovered, tunics are of appropriate colors, and the effect is childlike rather than realistic.

CASPAR, BALTHASAR, and MELCHIOR : Robes of rich material and colors of purple, gold, red, green, etc. Under the outside cloak a long tunic shows, caught with a wide girdle. Costumes should have a look of elegance, in contrast to SHEPHERDS, yet be easy and comfortable for the children to move in. (Old evening dresses, cloaks, and bathrobes from parents are most useful.) If those are not available, cotton flannel dyed, with borders, stripes, or designs painted on boldly, gives an excellent effect of depth and richness. Crowns can be made of papier-mâché or, if this is not possible, of stiff light cardboard painted gold and decorated with jewels. Flowing sleeves add to the dignity. Shoes can be suede sandals. They avoid clumping and help with good walk and carriage.

ATTENDANTS : Short tunics and tights like page boys. May have short capes. Bold colors can be used but must blend with the three kings. May have jaunty caps and wear sandals.

ARCHANGELS: Simple dress, soft full skirt, floor length, made of white nylon jersey or celanese—a material that falls in graceful folds as they walk, caught at the waist, with long, flowing pointed sleeves caught at the wrist. Large wings of buckram over wire, painted to look like feathers, are tied under the arms and around the waist through holes in the dresses. Gold collars, gold sandals, gold halos are used.

GREEN MEN OF THE WINTER SOLSTICE: Short green tunics and tights; green branches in their hats.

CHORUS: Over a nightgown or long slip, the girls wear floor-length tunics of a double layer of white cheesecloth. A hole is cut in the middle for the head. No sewing at the sides is necessary, but a white strip of cloth is around the waist, and a triangular kerchief of the same material is around the neck. Gold wings strategically placed and gold halos add greatly to the effect but must not hide a face. Sneakers are used.

The boys wear knee-length tunics of cotton flannel, hand dyed a wine red—with a hole in the middle for the head, a strip for a belt, and a piece of matching cloth for the neck. Use dark sweaters to cover the arms. The boys grasp in their right hands, just below the gold cross on the top, small gold rods (spears) that are shoulder height when they are seated. Sneakers are used.

IN A MANGER LAID

FAMILY: A comfortable farm family, circa 1900.

MOTHER and MARY: A long blue dress (the Virgin blue), tight bodice, buttoned in front, long sleeves with white ruching at neck and wrists; small white scarf around shoulders and small rose-colored apron; a halo for later scenes.

FATHER and JOSEPH: Red shirt, blue jeans, car-length sheepskin-lined coat; later a halo.

SARAH and RUTH: Full cotton dresses, high button boots of leatherette, and white stockings.

JOHN and SHEPHERDS: Blue jeans, fleece-lined jackets, knit mufflers, caps of gay colors (to look like American farm boys); crooks.

NARRATORS (if necessary): Dressed simply in quiet colors, like the boys and girls in the family—to tie in with the American scene.

GABRIEL: See The Prophecy in *Old Christmas.*

CHERRY TREE: Blue denim overalls, red shirt, bandanna. A small straw hat is effective but must not look funny.

HEROD, QUEEN, HARPER, CUP BEARER, ATTENDANTS, CHIEF PRIESTS, and SCRIBES: Rich colors and elegance befitting royalty and important people.

WISE MEN: Same as in other plays except high, twisted fantastic hats are substituted for crowns.

OX and ASS; CRÈCHE ANGELS and ARCHANGELS; and CHORUS: Same as in *Old Christmas.*

LARK, DOVE, OWL, and RED BIRD: Full, filmy dresses hanging straight from the shoulder; simple headdresses—bits of stiff material sewn to suggest beaks and little caps of cotton or fluff.

DOVE: Slate blue with a touch of pink; pink painted sandals.

LARK: Yellow with a touch of brown; yellow painted sandals.

RED BIRD: Red, with red painted sandals.

OWL: Brown, not as full or filmy as the others, with pointed bits of cloth sewn all over the dress to look like soft feathers.

All costumes are American except for ANGELS *who always look like angels, and* KINGS *who always look like kings, and courtiers from a distant land.*

BORN IN A STABLE

Prologue

In the dance pantomime to "The Virgin Unspotted"—

MARY: Filmy white dress and veil, something like china silk, that will float and fall gracefully as she dances; a halo; gold sandals.

JOSEPH: Floor-length brown tunic, not too narrow, as in play. Add a circular dark blue or black cape with a cherry red lining that, when held out at arms' length, forms a background for MARY and swirls as he dances.

The Play

MARY, JOSEPH, SHEPHERDS, KINGS, ATTENDANTS, OX, ASS, LAMB, ARCHANGEL, ANGELS OF THE CRÈCHE, CHORUS: Same as in *Old Christmas*.

INNKEEPERS, TAXPAYERS, JUGGLERS, TUMBLERS, and MAIDS: Skirts, tights, tunics, cloaks, shawls, hats, kerchiefs of gay colors, medieval in style.

APPLE TREE: Green tunic, red tights, and round wide red collar, cut in points.

GUARDING ANGEL: Dressed like ARCHANGELS—only smaller.

AUGUSTUS CAESAR: Long, elegant robe somewhat subdued in color and simple in line; plain gold circlet for crown.

HERALD: Tights, jerkin, and hat with feather, all in gay colors as befitting a very fine young gentleman.

PROPERTIES

Contributed by I. W. Seeley

THOSE USED IN ALL PLAYS

1. Star hung over the manger that allows for a light bulb inside, which makes a soft glow. May be obtained from the Moravian School in Salem, North Carolina.

2. Manger with straw

3. Stool for MARY

4. A rubber doll (the size comfortable for a child to hold), with a flat flashlight fixed firmly in it with tape, is used for the baby. The whole is wrapped in swaddling clothes, with the switch accessible and easy to manage. Soft trailing cheesecloth is draped over all so that the light is diffused. Rehearse the little virgin alone in the stable with the baby until she is at ease in holding, putting down, and picking up the baby and gets the light at the right angle to shine on her face.

5. Staff for JOSEPH

6. Crooks for the SHEPHERDS (as many as needed). Let them practice holding them away from the face and keeping them still.

7. Little pillows and blankets hidden in the straw for the animals to kneel on

8. Gifts for the SHEPHERDS to make—bird, lamb (piece of sheepskin folded and made to fit into the SHEPHERD's arms), etc.

9. Gifts of the three KINGS:

a. Gold—gild a box and fill it with pebbles (gilded and silvered)

119

and with ten-cent-store jewels. Must be grand to represent earthly treasure.

b. Frankincense—small pot on a chain that may be swung

c. Myrrh—a fair-sized dark vase of fine shape that can be carried with dignity

10. For the six ANGELS OF THE CRÈCHE (three on each side of stable roof):

Two gilded harps of plywood
Two gilded lutes of plywood
Two gilded trumpets of plywood. (Best effect is when the trumpets are next to the stable.)

OLD CHRISTMAS

The Prophecy

Five big open flat books for PROPHETS. (SIXTH PROPHET has none.)
Sewing for MARY that can be slipped into pocket
Lily for GABRIEL
Straw for the roof of the stable and for floor inside

IN A MANGER LAID

For Family Scene

Everything must be small to be in proportion and give the general appearance of a comfortable, cozy farmhouse—not too distinctly one part of the country.

Table—with a cover preferably with tassels, books, and a bowl of holly
A few chairs—Early American—one with arms for FATHER
Rug
Christmas tree (optional)
Staff and knife for JOHN
Knitting and sewing for MOTHER and SARAH and RUTH

Bible for FATHER to read from

Lily for GABRIEL

The cherry tree—bare branch with the smallest red Christmas tree
  balls and a few light green paper leaves tied on

Crown for HEROD

Circlet for the QUEEN

Flowers for tiaras for the ladies

Scroll for CHIEF PRIEST

Harp or American dulcimer for HARPER

Rod with gold hanging to be carried by two pages to indicate
  throne

Stool carried by two ladies for QUEEN to sit near HEROD

BORN IN A STABLE

Roman circlet and plain scepter for AUGUSTUS CAESAR

Scroll

Rugs, pitchers, etc., for MAIDS

Earthenware bowl for grain for ox, ASS, and LAMB

Bundles, etc., of all colors for TAXPAYERS

Recorder

Papier-mâché mugs and two big bowls for wassailers

APPLE TREE—bare branch or *small* tree with red paper apples tied
  on, with some extras to pelt audience with as they run off

For JUGGLERS, rubber balls painted like oranges

Hammer and plank for JAMES

Cake, crock of butter, etc., anything homely for gifts from the
  people to the baby

Small bundle for MARY

LIGHTING

Contributed by Diana King

While it would be possible to perform the Christmas plays without stage lights, even minimal lighting will enhance their beauty out of all proportion to the amount of trouble and expense involved. Often there is someone who knows about lighting who can advise.

If the lighting changes are not to be distracting, a dimmer is essential for the gradual raising and lowering of the lights.

The plays do not call for elaborate lighting changes. At the beginning of the plays, the ANGEL CHORUS enters in the dark. As soon as they are all in place, the lights are raised gradually. In general, start with soft lighting and lower all lights before the crèche doors are opened. MARY and child are, at first, only lit with a soft glow; nothing else is visible, so that the effect is one of mystery and intimacy. Following the crèche scene, the lights are brought up slowly, ending in a blaze of brilliance reminiscent of a Botticelli nativity.

At The Potomac School, we are fortunate in possessing extensive lighting equipment, acquired over a long period of time. We use the following to light the play:

1. Border lights (white, amber, and blue). We have no footlights.

2. Two 500-watt Lekos to light the CHORUS banked high at either side of the stage

3. Two 1000-watt spots to light the proscenium, the family scene in the American play, etc. These could with advantage be replaced with the more modern Lekos.

4. Two 500-watt Fresnels to light the stage area. These give a very soft light, almost devoid of shadow.

5. Two 400-watt spots to light the CRÈCHE ANGELS on either side of the stable

6. Star, lit with several 15-watt bulbs

7. Christmas tree bulb slightly darkened with paint to light the stable

All except the last are attached to a dimmer.

Stage lighting equipment can often be rented. However, it is important to reserve whatever is needed well ahead of time as rental equipment is often in great demand at Christmas. Should it be deemed wiser to buy the equipment, about two hundred dollars would suffice for the initial outlay. Several good books on stage lighting are available from most public libraries.

We prepare our lighting scripts with great care, recording all changes in the margin of the play itself and keeping records of lighting from year to year. As soon as the play is ready to be rehearsed all the way through, lights should be added. Many changes are often necessary, even at the last minute. It should be remembered that costumes affect the amount of light reflected. The children have to become used to the lights. The glare of the lights prevents the actors and singers from seeing the audience, thereby making them less self-conscious. It is, however, important to caution children against gazing directly into the lights.

While changes in lighting provide for variety in brightness, their most important effect is in their power to change the size of the picture, providing movement, much as a camera does in ranging between closeups and distant shots. By changing lighting, it is possible to focus the attention of the audience on a single figure or on the stage as a whole.

STAGING

Contributed by Helen M. Seth-Smith

There should be one person in charge of all plans for stage construction, someone who can work with the carpenter, handyman, and any extra help, and who can also work closely with the producer.

We are including sketches, diagrams, and photographs showing different ways of achieving settings and hope that these suggestions may aid and ease the giving of a very beautiful and unusual Christmas play.

The scenery at The Potomac School was painted each year by older children as part of their art work. The play was read and, with the art teacher and director, the requirements discussed. There were questions and answers concerning points for emphasis, period, limitations imposed by lighting, costumes, space, entrances, exits, etc. Each pupil made a sketch for consideration. Parts from different sketches were chosen to be put together or an especially good one taken, but all had the benefit of constructive criticism. Under the direction of the art teacher, committees were formed and work was under way. The result was nearly always delightful, in addition to being good experience.

When scenery was not used, a small stable was constructed and placed at the back, in the middle of the stage. The children banked the background with greens fastened through chicken wire. Screens covered with greens or small trees shielded exits. The effect was pleasing, Christmasy, and deliciously fragrant.

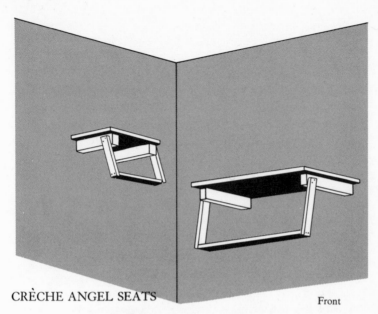

CRÈCHE ANGEL SEATS

Front

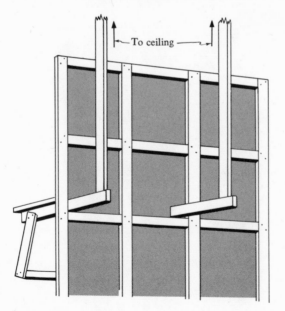

To ceiling

Back

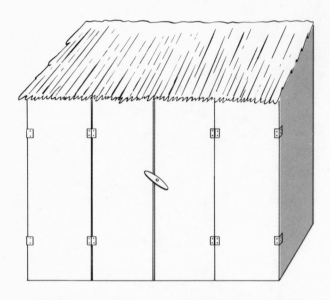

THE STABLE SHOWING THE FOLDING DOORS

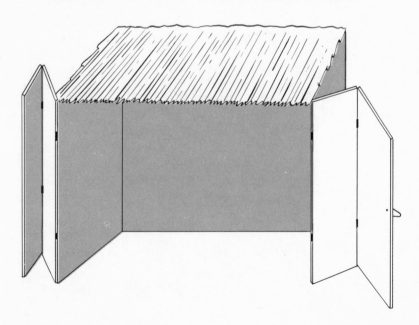

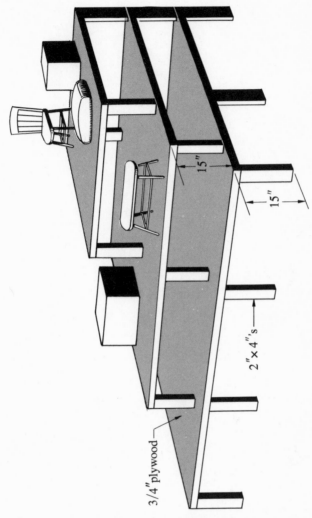

Angel chorus heights. These basic heights are built on top of the main platforms either side of the stage. If blocks, cushions, small chairs, etc., are safely placed on these sturdy heights, attractive and interesting groupings can be made to give the illusion of "angels in the sky."

Appendix

A SUGGESTED LIST
OF APPROPRIATE MUSIC
AND ITS USE FOR EACH PLAY

1. "The First Nowell" ("The First Noël")
   Sung by the audience before each play begins while CHORUS
   enters. No. 27, *Oxford Book of Carols,* Oxford University
   Press, London, but it is such a familiar tune that it can be
   found in any hymnal. A good descant is published by
   H. W. Gray, New York.

OLD CHRISTMAS

2. "Veni Emmanuel"—No. 2, *The Hymnal of the Protestant
   Episcopal Church in the United States of America, 1940,* Church
   Pension Fund, New York
   or "Divinum Mysterium" ("Of the Father's Love Begotten")—
   No. 20, *The Hymnal of the Protestant Episcopal Church in the
   United States of America, 1940*
3. "Nova, Nova"—*Musica Britannica,* Volume IV, Stainer and Bell
   Ltd., London (Galaxy Music Corp., New York, American agent)
   or "Nowell, Carol of Salutation"—*Musica Britannica*, Volume IV
4. "Puer Nobis" ("Unto Us a Boy Is Born")—No. 92, *Oxford Book
   of Carols*
5. "Sussex Carol" ("On Christmas Night")—No. 24, *Oxford Book
   of Carols*
   or "Alleluia Round"—by William Boyce, in *The Recorder Guide*
   by Joanna E. Kulbach and Arthur Nitka, Oak Publications, Inc.,
   New York
6. "Lo, How a Rose E'er Blooming"—16th century melody, harmonized, by Praetorius, E. C. Schirmer Music Company, Boston

131

7. "The Moon Shines Bright"—*Folk-Song Carols* collected and arranged by Cecil J. Sharp, Novello & Co. Ltd., London (H. W. Gray Company, New York, American agent)
   or "The Bellman's Song"—No. 46, *Oxford Book of Carols*

8. "While By My Sheep"—*Christmas Carols From Many Countries*, arranged by Satis N. Coleman and Elin R. Jörgensen, G. Schirmer, Inc., New York

9. "Sing Aloud on This Day!" ("Personent Hodie")—No. 78, *Oxford Book of Carols*

10. "Upon My Lap My Sovereign Sits"—by Martin Peerson, E. C. Schirmer. If desired, accompaniment for three strings is included with the three parts for SSA voices.
    or "This Endris Night"—No. 39, *Oxford Book of Carols*

11. "Coventry Carol" ("Lully, Lulla")—No. 22, *Oxford Book of Carols*

12. "In Dulci Jubilo"—No. 86, *Oxford Book of Carols*
    or "Tomorrow Shall Be My Dancing Day" — No. 71, *Oxford Book of Carols*

13. "The Holly and the Ivy"—No. 38, *Oxford Book of Carols*

14. "Masters in This Hall"—arranged by Gustav Holst, J. Curwen & Sons, London (G. Schirmer, Inc., American agent); reprinted in the *Oxford Book of Carols,* No. 137
    or "Welcome Yule"—No. 174, *Oxford Book of Carols*

IN A MANGER LAID

15. "Wondrous Love"—arranged by Annabel Buchanan for *Twelve Folk Hymns,* edited by John Powell, J. Fischer & Bro., Glen Rock, New Jersey

16. "Jesus Born in Bethlea"—*Twelve Folk Hymns*

17. "Seven Joys of Mary"—arranged by John Jacob Niles, G. Schirmer (traditional Tennessee)

18. "The Cherry Tree Carol"—arranged by Hilton Rufty, J. Fischer & Bro. (traditional Kentucky)

19. "The Babe of Bethlehem"—*Twelve Folk Hymns*
20. "My Shepherd Will Supply My Need"—arranged by Virgil Thompson, H. W. Gray Company
21. "Go Tell It on the Mountain"—arranged by John W. Work, Galaxy Music Corp. (traditional Negro)
22. "Star in the East" ("Hail the Blest Morn")—based on a Kentucky version of the folk-hymn, as sung by Mrs. Rachel Ritchie, E. C. Schirmer
23. "Ancient Moravian Christmas Carol"—by Christian Gregor, 1783; arranged by Harvey Gaul, Galaxy Music Corp.

BORN IN A STABLE

24. "This Is the Truth Sent from Above"—arranged by R. Vaughan Williams, Stainer and Bell Ltd., London; reprinted in the *Oxford Book of Carols,* No. 68
25. "The Virgin Unspotted"—*Folk-Song Carols,* collected and arranged by Cecil J. Sharp, Novello & Co. Ltd. (H. W. Gray Company, American agent)
    or "A Virgin Most Pure"—No. 4, *Oxford Book of Carols*
    or "In Bethlehem City"—*Folk Songs of the Four Seasons,* arranged by R. Vaughan Williams, Oxford University Press, London
26. "Christmas Eve"—No. 1, *Oxford Book of Carols* (English)
27. "Gloucestershire Wassail"—No. 31, *Oxford Book of Carols*
    or "Wassail, Wassail!"—*Christmas Carols from Many Countries* collected by Satis N. Coleman and Elin K. Jörgensen, G. Schirmer
28. "Apple Tree Wassail"—*Folk Songs from Somerset,* Fifth Series, collected by Cecil Sharp
29. "Hosanna"—*L'Enfance du Christ* by Berlioz, Costallat, Paris
30. "Ding-Dong! Merrily on High"—melody Branle de L'Official (from Thoinot Arbeau's Orchesographie, 1588), E. C. Schirmer
31. "Lo, How a Rose"—arranged as a canon by C. Vulpius, 1600

or "There Is No Rose of Such Vertu"—*Musica Britannica,* Volume IV, anon. 1425 (for those experienced)
    or "Greensleeves"—No. 28, *Oxford Book of Carols*
32. "Lullay My Liking"—No. 182, *Oxford Book of Carols*
33. "Christ Child's Lullaby"—music arranged by Marjory Kennedy-Fraser, words from Father Allan MacDonald, noted in Eriskay from the singing of Mrs. John Macinnes, from *Songs of the Hebrides,* Vol. I, Boosey and Hawkes, New York (for more experienced voices)
34. "Somerset Carol"—No. 8, *Oxford Book of Carols*
    or "Alleluia Round"—by William Boyce, Oak Publications, Inc.
35. "Sussex Mummers' Carol"—No. 45, *Oxford Book of Carols*
    or "Sing Aloud on This Day!"—No. 78, *Oxford Book of Carols*

Where a chorus or instruments for live music are not available, some good records such as the following—with a little skill and the help of tape recorders for cuts—can be used to great advantage at appropriate places. Also, these records can be used to familiarize the cast with this kind of music. All contain carols suggested for the plays and should be obtainable through any good record shop. If other records are used—and there are a number—choose carefully to find those that are appropriate for plays such as these. Try to avoid hymns, which are better in church services.

For *Old Christmas* and *Born in a Stable*
 1. *A Festival of Lessons and Carols,* No. 5523
As sung in King's College Chapel, Cambridge, England, upon Christmas Eve 1958 (Boys' and men's voices)
 2. *A Procession with Carols,* No. 5651
By the same choir (Boys' and men's voices)
 3. *A Ceremony of Carols,* set by Benjamin Britten, R. O. 179
Sung by the choristers of Canterbury Cathedral, England. Printed by Argo Record Co., Ltd., 113 Fulham Road, London, S.W. 3

4. *Christmas Hymns and Carols,* No. LM 2139, Vol. 1, RCA Victor
Sung by the Robert Shaw Chorale (Mixed adult voices; album contains some hymns, which should not be used)
5. *Joy to the World,* P8353, Capitol
Sung by the Roger Wagner Chorale (Mixed adult voices; album contains some hymns, which should not be used)
6. *Noel—French Noels of the XVII and XVIII Centuries*
Performed on the Silbermann Organ in the Abby Church, Marmoutier, Alsace, France—Melville Smith, Organist. Cambridge Records, P. O. Box 262, Bedford, Massachusetts (These lively old tunes played on this ancient organ have the sounds of bells and wind instruments.)

For *In a Manger Laid*
1. *Carols of All Seasons,* No. TLP 1031
Sung by Jean Richie, a traditional singer. Printed by Tradition Records, Box 72, Village Station, New York, N.Y. 10014

For *Born in a Stable*
1. *Christmas Music*
Sung by the children of The Potomac School, directed by John Langstaff. Privately issued in 1966 and obtainable from The Potomac School, P.O. Box 430, McLean, Virginia 22101